Once Upon A Dream

Kent Dream Weavers

Edited By Warren Arthur

First published in Great Britain in 2017 by:

Young Writers
Remus House
Coltsfoot Drive
Peterborough
PE2 9BF
Telephone: 01733 890066
Website: www.youngwriters.co.uk

Book Design by Spencer Hart

SB ISBN 978-1-78820-390-6
Printed and bound in the UK by BookPrintingUK
Website: www.bookprintinguk.com
YB0333M

FOREWORD

Welcome Readers!

Dreams play a big role in our life, whether from the worlds that keep us entertained at night to the dreams and ambitions we aspire to in the future, so it was only fitting we used this as our topic for our latest nationwide primary school competition.

I am proud to present 'Once Upon A Dream – Kent Dream Weavers', a collection of poetic treasures that will make your imaginations run wild. Among these pages you will find a variety of poetic styles, from dream acrostics to candy land couplets to fear provoking free verse. Some poems may leave you jumping for joy, some may tickle your sides, while others may pull at your heartstrings as each author becomes their own dream catcher.

The selection process, while difficult, proved to be a very rewarding task and I hope you enjoy the range of work that has made it to the final stages. With so many wonderful poems featured in this anthology picking a winner was another very difficult task so well done to *Ruth Yates* who has been chosen as the best poet. I'd also like to congratulate all the young writers featured in this collection.

Finally, I hope you find the poems that lie within these pages just as entertaining as I did and I hope it is kept as a keepsake for many years to come.

Warren Arthur

CONTENTS

Valley Invicta Primary School At Holborough Lakes, Snodland

Wellesley House, Broadstairs

THE POEMS

Well done! Your poem has been chosen as the best in this book.

Magic Garden Adventure!

One night while I was sleeping
I had a strange surprise
I felt myself drift away
And saw a magic garden right before my eyes.

It was magical but frightening
So I squeezed my sister's hand
There were feathery birds
And dancing fairies throughout this gleaming land.

We both slid down a grassy slope
Then everything went dark
I found myself in a lonely cave
And saw we'd been spread apart.

Through the gloomy cave I crept
And saw a bottle lying there
I picked it up and looked inside
But spilt it everywhere.

I felt extremely frightened
As bats circled around my head
The land started swaying
And I found I was safe in bed.

Ruth Yates (8)
Tubbenden Primary School, Orpington

When I Grow Up

When I grow up
I dream of being a swimmer.
I dream of being a teacher.
I dream of being a nurse.
I dream of being a chef.
I dream of being a Power Ranger.
I dream of building Lego.
I dream of talking on the telephone.
I dream of being a princess
And I dream of being a doctor.

Brooke, Grace (11), Rebecca, Maab, Abdi, Joshua, Charlotte, David (10) & Abbie
Marjorie McClure School, Chislehurst

Dream

D addy dog pushed the door to the dinosaur disco to dance with a digger duck.
R ain rangers ran through the rainbow with the rhino rabbit.
E lephants eat eye-gazes.
A dorable alligators ate the apples.
M arvellous monkey wants more of the massive magic map.

Joshua, Evie Nickells (6), Charlotte, David (10), Grace (11), Abbie, Abdi, Rebecca, Maab, Brooke & Izzy (8)
Marjorie McClure School, Chislehurst

Our Dreams

Last night I dreamt about a princess' castle,
A new house,
Being on a computer with snakes everywhere,
Butterflies,
Being a superhero and saving everyone,
Toys,
Brushing my hair and teeth and having a shower,
Being a tiger and going swimming in a cloud.

Brooke, Grace (11), Rebecca, Maab, Abdi, Joshua, Charlotte, David (10) & Abbie
Marjorie McClure School, Chislehurst

A Dream

A big burger.
A giant chocolate cake.
A piece of Lego.
A television.
A SpongeBob bed.
A holiday.
A friend.
A dream.

Joshua (7), Evie Nickells (6), Charlotte, Abdi, David Wang (10), Maab & Grace (11)
Marjorie McClure School, Chislehurst

Once Upon A Dream

T he spooky, scary spider forest, I thought it was a myth.
H ere I am, the spider forest and I'm scared stiff.
E ventually, I'll be eaten.

S neaking through the forest, watching my every step,
P eople like me are scared of spiders, especially the cobwebs.
I can see all the cobwebs, closing their sticky eyes,
D eadly spiders roaming, and hiding like little spies.
E very breath I take here, it gets more silent,
R esonating through the echoes of fear and violence.
S o I find a spiderweb gate, oh great!

F ear expands around my body and forces me to touch the gate
O ptimistically I poke it, with a thud behind me I meet my fate!
R avenously, a hairy, slick, slimy spider scoops me,
E ventually I am on a cobweb and I can't flee.
S o the spider starts licking me, I just want to flop.
T urns out my dog was licking, so please, please stop!

Heyes Gearing (9)
Smarden Primary School, Smarden

Once Upon A Dream/A Magical Night!

I was walking in the wood
As fast as I could,
The wood was scary,
Apparently there were bears.
I was walking my French bulldog,
Suddenly, everything was fog!
Lucy the dog panicked.
We couldn't see!
'Argh!' We fell in a pit
And I took a hit.
I went into a coma
And then into a dream...
'Urgh!' I woke up with a bump
And had a sore rump!
My eyes focused,
I saw a lilac fairy!
She was as pretty as a flower.
I wonder if she had any power?
I asked her questions,
She gave me lessons,
She helped me out the hole,
She was very kind,

She took me for a fly,
We went so high!
We went over the lake
And saw a unicorn!
She was having a drink,
Her name was Twink.
She looked as pretty as soft candyfloss.
We soared down to the ground.
We said, 'Hello,'
And played together,
We fought
And thought,
Until we had an idea -
Let's write a nonsense poem.
It goes: The song song,
Silly sausages sung.
The Holland horse hollered.
Help! Holly hit Helen,
Hannah hollered.
Calum Cow caught a cold!
That's the farm song!
Yippee! Our poem was famous,
Lots of money for us...

Next we met the Queen
She was supreme.
She invited us to her party...
It's a ball
In a very big hall...
We had such a good time
The food was divine,
We had so much fun
Now the day is done.
But I hear pop music,
I open my eyes to see my dog
Dancing in her bikini
With her boyfriends.

Elizabeth Rose Kenneally (10)
Smarden Primary School, Smarden

Once Upon A Dream

One day in Smarden as I fell asleep
I had a wonderful dream.
My uncle's dog and I
That is the breed called Dogue de Bordeaux,
He ran out then I said, 'No!'
As we glided through the air Duck died
And he went like he just didn't care.
My eyes sparkled as I went through the sky.

We went to Eco Point, Antarctica,
I saw machine guns and home-made buns.

Bang!
Zeus hit a tower about 100 foot in the air.
Then fell down to the stony, snowy ground.
My blood sank into my boots.

I thought he was dead so I called Ted
Who is his vet.

We picked up Zeus and he was as good as new.
We picked up Mercy, Roadhog, Tracer
And Soldier and they killed Zeus.
But Mercy revived him but I still...
Woke up crying and screaming
And Zeus lived forever.

Harry Anthony Howard-Hollingsbee (10)
Smarden Primary School, Smarden

Once Upon A Dream

M onday was the day my cat and its kitten bravely beat up a robber,
Y es you heard me, my cat beat up a robber!

S hape-shifted into a human, did my cat,
H e tripped up the robber for the police.
A s he did, he shape-shifted back,
P olice, well they were amazed,
E ven though they have no idea, of who it was,

S o the police smashed through bins, making them do somersaults,
H iding away was my breathtaking cat and his kitten,
I n more details his name is Smokey and the kitten is Garfield.
F inding them was a real pain for the police,
T heir perseverance did pay off, they never found them.
I n the end he came back to the police in human form
N ow listen here, you won't believe it, he got one million pound.
G oing to a shop with that he brought a lifelong stash of cat treats.

C ompletely happy he went back home,
A fter coming home he snooped around the house,
T o make sure no one saw his stash of cat treats.

D aydreaming he ate a piece of brown choco fudge cake,
R unning up the stairs he was tired and exhausted after the day he'd had.
E verywhere around were stars, which were making him sleepy,
A nd Garfield was terribly tired and felt like he could not move,
M aking his way to his bed, he fell straight asleep curled up in a ball.

Finn Goodwin (10)
Smarden Primary School, Smarden

Once Upon A Dream

It couldn't get much better than this,
All I did was make a wish.
I closed my eyes to see the light,
And I got such a wonderful fright.
It was half-time of the match,
And all I just want was a patch.
To make sure I was alright,
As it was the Champions League final tonight.

I was playing very well indeed
But what I didn't know was how I hurt my knee.
I had a cruciate ligament injury.
There was a person acting aggressive,
Who made me feel I needed to do something impressive.
Before I got that nasty thing,
I quickly went over to the bin,
I also saved a goal,
It flew quickly like a troll.
But unfortunately for me,
I could not see.
I would never play again,
I had to stick with writing with a pen.

Thankfully I woke up safe, lying in bed,
I knew it wasn't real as I could see my teddy, Ted.
But wait a second, oh no, it's not real,
I don't know how it wasn't a big deal,
For I couldn't get it out of my head,
I need to go back to bed!

Will Barber (11)
Smarden Primary School, Smarden

Once Upon A Dream...

I have two brains tonight,
It gives me quite a fright!
All around is smoke,
It's definitely no joke!
Then, out of the gloom
I realise I am in a room.

Then I see my good dreams fall,
The bad dreams have won, this isn't right at all!
Then I think I am in a giant's tummy,
OMG! He must feel like a mummy!
Then, while the other monsters aren't looking,
I find two steaks and begin the cooking!
The giant does a horrible, belchy burp
And a terrible, squelchy slurp!

And off I zoom,
Past the moon!
Then I feel a blizzard
And out scampers a jolly, old wizard.

Pip, pop, boom, shed!
Now I know I am back in bed.
I nearly have a fit,

It is just getting to the best bit!
The only good dream I'd have today,
Is about that good wizard blasting away.

Ruby Parkman (10)
Smarden Primary School, Smarden

Once Upon A Dream

Now this is a poem about my dreams,
Where nothing is really what it seems.
Now I hope you're not getting bored,
You are? OK then, let's get on with the poem.

I was in hospital one day,
And my mind drifted away,
Like an astronaut in outer space,
Forgetting his rightful place.
Down on Earth below,
Where he started to know,
What life was all about.

Suddenly I was in the woods,
Listening to the trees,
Whistling along with the birds,
Then I saw Evil running through the trees,
Leaving broken dreams behind wherever he goes.

And this reason nobody knows,
Evil Mr Fantasy steals your dreams,
But no one knows he's not what he seems!

Thud! I woke up on the hospital floor,
Surrounded by doctors
And nurses and more.
It was just a dream!

Evie Williamson (10)
Smarden Primary School, Smarden

Once Upon A Dream

One day a boy called Leon
Was with his friends Jack and Bobby.
They went to the park and found a secret passageway.
They also found a portal.
They decided to jump into the portal.
Then they went to the fair
But the people were aliens and the portal disappeared.

'Where did it go?' said Jack.
'I don't know,' said Bob.
The aliens stared at them,
As we were the weird ones.
They saw a roller coaster.

So they went on the roller coaster.
Instead of forward it went backwards and was on fire.
When they got off there was a loud rumble.
Crack! 'Argh!
Monsters, run!' shouted Jack.
The monsters chased them
And surrounded them in a corner.
A magical wizard saved them.
He teleported them back home
And made them forget that day.

Leon Kennaird (9)
Smarden Primary School, Smarden

Once Upon A Dream

As I fell asleep I arrived in my house
Playing with my toys
I saw my dog Truffy sitting.
She got up, jumped out the window,
She span and zoomed off like a rocket in the sky.
Bang!

We had crashed
And I got my knee bashed.
We had landed on an island.
The sky blackened.
It was a place called Route 66 in mid-air.
We acted like we just didn't care.

I saw guns and a man making guns,
There was lots of fighting and biting.
There were people called Soldier 76,
McCree, Mercy and Roadhog
Fighting Coniggly, Hog, Bottom Squiffler
And Widdling Biff.
Truffy flew up and Soldier 76 said,
'Get out of here, it's not safe!'
So Truffy flew down back to Earth
And I woke up out of my dream.

Caleb Underdown (10)
Smarden Primary School, Smarden

Once Upon A Dream

S he is my imaginary unicorn,
T hat can fly. She makes me happy,
A nd as free as can be,
R ound the moon and stars we go,

T hat shimmer in the sky,
H ow could we ever go wrong,
E ating away at the sugary grass,

M ouths are moving, munching away,
A nd gazing up at the stars,
G iggling at the sound of the waves,
I swiftly jumped on and gallop off,
C an't believe it, I can fly...
A nd with that, I let go,
L iving the ultimate dream,

U nder the moon we go,
N ow down to the sea we go,
I laugh,
C ry,
O ther things,
R ound to the land,
N ever to see Star again.

Lara Jayne Town (11)
Smarden Primary School, Smarden

Once Upon A Dream

Whoosh! I'm soaring through the atmosphere,
Sadly this had always been my greatest fear.

With a wizzle and a wazzle
I could nearly reach the moon.
Since I was there I knew I'd be there soon.
With a jiggle and a joggle, I was halfway to Mars,
Space is really beautiful because of all the stars.

I was halfway through a wormhole,
When I saw a big black mole.
I thought that was rather odd,
Seeing as I was eating cod.

Cod was not my favourite food
And just as I said that I heard a cow go 'lood'!
Which I thought was rather rude,
Seeing as it could have just mooed.

Then, all of a sudden I crashed my ship.
Then of course, I just woke up.
It was just a dream.

Jake Robinson (10)
Smarden Primary School, Smarden

Once Upon A Dream

Me and Catty walking down streets,
Suddenly we see red blood seats.

We sit on a giant, fat, wooden hand
And on the ground is some white creamy sand.
Bang! Twiz! and a pat!
Woo! I'm flying, look at that!

Flying, landing on the road,
I see a cushion brightly sewed.

I see a hotel way down,
I look at it and start to beam.
We go in and book a room
And find a very brown, broken broom.

Catty and me start to sweep
And at the same time we leap.

Fun and games all day long,
Now it's time to sing a lovely song.

'You're tired,' you said,
'So let's hurry up and go to bed.'

Georgia Edmed (10)
Smarden Primary School, Smarden

Once Upon A Dream

M onsters under my bed singing so little boys come to die.
Y ellow blobs jump, jump, jump across my bed.
T he dinos cry about tiny mosquitoes.
H issing comes from behind my curtain.
I don't think I'm dreaming, this seems very real!
C ats flying all over the place.
A nimals try to fit in a suitcase.
L lamas eating a shoelace.

R ight, this isn't a dream
E ven though it feels like one
V illains steal pets and say, 'Argh!'
E verywhere I go there's funky monkeys.
R hinos charge at trees.
I am in a moving bed.
E ven though I fell and hit my head.

Kaiden Parfitt (9)
Smarden Primary School, Smarden

Once Upon A Dream

(Inspired by 'On The Ning Nang Nong' by Spike Milligan)

On the Bing Bang Bong
Where the duck went dong
And the dog goes wiffer, waffer, woo
On the Bong Bing Bang
Where the cow goes clang
And all the pigs go plipper, plopper, ploo
On the Bang Bong Bing
Where the cat goes ping
And the spiders eat the sugary, sour sweets.

On the Drake, Dring, Drong
Where the people never sing
And the mice are never ever happy
On the Drake, Drang, Dring
Where the fairies never ping
And the horse is as sad as ever
On the Drong, Drang, Drake
Where the pigs go quake
But at that moment I realise
I'm awake!

Megan O'Rourke (10)
Smarden Primary School, Smarden

Once Upon A Dream

I had just fallen asleep.
I was walking in Bing Bong City
With my favourite best friends,
Will Barber and Harry Hollingsbee.
We were walking into Bingka Forest,
It is private.

As we strolled through Bingka Forest
We saw awesome ting tang trees.
I thought that something really bad
Was gonna happen.
I was sad.
Suddenly we could see smog or fog.

Will saw a platymouse, it attacked us.
It wouldn't stop attacking
More and more but...
Then I woke up.
What a horrible dream.

Joshua Michael Underdown (10)
Smarden Primary School, Smarden

Once Upon A Dream

S eeing something in my haunted house,
C lenching my best friend's hands,
A rching my back in a weird way,
R ed spots coming out of the mist,
Y earning as I shiver in fear.

M urky shadows appearing slowly,
O nly my fear is burning up,
N earing and nearing, my tension rising up,
S piders hanging everywhere,
T ensing up as a spider crawls down my back,
E ven my friend is scared,
R eaching out for some help, nothing happens, I am dead!

Millie Allen (11)
Smarden Primary School, Smarden

Once Upon A Dream!

H orrid nightmare
O ne big, green, bristly giant
R unning as quick as I can from the bristly beast
R oaring and thudding after me
O ver the playground we go
R unning round from the school thinking I'd lost him!

D reaming of getting eaten
R ed raspberry blood
E ating and chomping, wait I'm in a tummy
A ngrily trying to get out
M um will be wondering where me, the midget is!

Gracie Patricia Ella Hanson (10)
Smarden Primary School, Smarden

Once Upon A Dream

Once there was a wizard, very small,
He could do the most wildest things of all,
Like making teddy bears talk
And even make them walk.
He made a stork that could snort
And a snail that could make you frail.

The wizard could make pigs grow wings
And a dog with frogs' legs that sings.
He could give someone a million sweets
And a big treat.
He could fly and make someone cry, even you
And goodness knows what else he could do!

Oliver Holton (10)
Smarden Primary School, Smarden

Once Upon A Dream

H ad the worst dream last night
O f course I wasn't scared,
R unning through the woods.
R apidly howling out for help.
O ver the top of the cliff, I heard a noise.
R unning for my life, I had no time for toys.

D reaming I prayed
R unning through the woods
E nd of it all
A nd breaking the rules
M y bed! Yes, I'm back.

Hollie Kitney (10)
Smarden Primary School, Smarden

Nightmares

N o one is in this smoke-filled land,
I see nothing but pitch-black sand.
G rey sunlight falls upon the light,
H igh up in the sky the moon gives a fright.
T onight the moon hangs low.
M y eyes move very slowly.
A sound like thunder comes from the right,
R ays of light come from above.
E verywhere there is smoke and sometimes a beam,
S tupidly there are two moons, wait, this isn't a dream!

Callum Gregory (10)
Staplehurst School, Staplehurst

Gliding Across The Sky

As I step onto my unicorn we start to take flight.
I cuddle onto his velvet fur as we fly through the night.
We land in a valley of clouds, white is all I can see.
Other small unicorns, it's a lovely place to be.
My unicorn flies around, he's giving me a tour.
There's King Candy's castle guarded by ogres,
I really want to see more.
We start to fly up high,
I love it with my unicorn
When we're gliding across the sky.

Robin Taylor (10)
Staplehurst School, Staplehurst

Super-Dude

I'm at college,
My belly full of porridge,
Dark Sing, aka Miss Masson, strikes,
I turn into...
Super-Dude!

I put on my pants,
Make sure there are no ants.
They're over my trousers,
Stick on my symbol and mask,
I'm now...
Super-Dude!

My powers are speed and flight.
I'm rarely found at night.
I fight Dark Sing and I...
Pow! Crash! Bang! Vroom!
I'm in bed.

Jack Coleridge (9)
Staplehurst School, Staplehurst

Woodlice Can Be Scary!

A woodlouse as big as a boulder,
I can see it over my shoulder,
Running away so I won't be flat.
Good thing I'm not wearing a hat,
Hired some builders to make a ramp,
There in the road I stare at a tramp.
The woodlouse goes up the ramp
And leaves with a bang!

Somehow the woodlouse can still hang.

I open my eyes with a gleam
Until I realise it is just a dream.

Anthony Wilson (10)
Staplehurst School, Staplehurst

Impossible

I mpossible creatures
M agical creatures
P inky, sharky; pink shark
O inky doggy; pig dog
S nake lady; half snake, half lady
S nake man, you know what I mean
I ce cream shark; shark made of ice cream
B ig bad babies, with wings of steel
L ollipop snake, ready for the meal
E very one of them are fake.

Ciaran Clark (10)
Staplehurst School, Staplehurst

The Animal Athletes

The lion roars through his whistle.
The fox is late and all the animals have gone.
The gorilla swings through the vines.
The monkey was not far behind.
The cheetah is in the lead,
But we forgot he can't go far.
The bunny goes through her underground burrow.
The panther sprints past the zoo.
The bunny wins.
Bang!
She wakes back in her old boring hutch.

Hannah Gilmore (9)
Staplehurst School, Staplehurst

Unicorns

U nder my bed I hide and wait
N othing is coming, maybe it's late
I waited for ages until I heard something
C ould it be him?
O h no! Here he comes!
R ampaging horned beast holding currant buns
N othing can stop him, what do I do?
S uddenly I wake up and all I can say is, 'Phew!'

Lauren Louise Lawson (9)
Staplehurst School, Staplehurst

Pounce!

Fairies fly and flutter in the sky,
Flowers sway every which way,
Mermaids swim like dolphins full of joy.
Meanwhile, the devil is doing its job.
When leaves fall down, so do stars
And there go all your hopes and dreams,
All at once!
The gullible grouch is still in its cave,
Just waiting for the perfect moment to pounce!

Elodie LeGrande (10)
Staplehurst School, Staplehurst

Weather

W hen the animals are wild the weather is mild.
E ars are warm and animals are born.
A mother covers the babies in their warmth.
T hey sometimes live in fresh straw, they lay.
H orses poo every day.
E xaggerating clean-ups before summer days.
R ight places for every day!

Phoenix Santer (10)
Staplehurst School, Staplehurst

Dragons

D eep in the forest something lurks inside,
R oaring and screaming nightmares have arrived,
A t my feet... a dragon awakes,
G lancing left and right, all I see is smoke,
O h my, is this meant to be a joke?
N ightmares have surrounded me,
S uddenly, I awoke!

Jessica Somauroo (10)
Staplehurst School, Staplehurst

Animals

A n animal scampers about
N aked mole rats creep
I n a cave lurk some bats
M ammals like to laze about
A nd the rhino over there snorts
L ong-legged hawk eagle soars and claws
S uddenly a cheetah runs, then it fades, it's just a dream!

Jesper Axel Kennedy Russell (9)
Staplehurst School, Staplehurst

The Race

And the moon blows his whistle,
And the planets storm off,
The stars cheer and shout,
Earth charges ahead,
Around the sun,
They dodge and dart between meteors,
The stars shout and cheer,
As they come to an end the winner is clear...
Earth.

Maddie Simpson (10)
Staplehurst School, Staplehurst

Fantastic

F airies and witches
A nts and stitches
N arnia and beans
T antrums and ice creams
A liens and butter
S andwiches and stutter
T ea and rats
I nk and bats
C ats and dreams.

Boglarka Tollas (10)
Staplehurst School, Staplehurst

You Can Be Anything

I want to be a unicorn.
It would be a perfect dream.
Faster than fairies, faster than bees.
Rainbow hair, pretty as can be.
Swirling ice cream cone horn
With beautiful purple fur.

'Urgh!'
My alarm.

Amelie Clements (9)
Staplehurst School, Staplehurst

The Bunny Ballerina Dream

Hunny the bunny leaps around the room.
Hunny the bunny dives past Ms Loop.
Hunny the bunny skips through the hoop.
Hunny the bunny dances to France.
Finds her true love.
Pow!
She is up and her love is gone.

Jasmine Schlosser (10)
Staplehurst School, Staplehurst

Nightmare

I get stuck in a spooky room,
There's no escape at all,
It is dark and gloomy
And I'm trapped all by myself,
Water's filling up,
I start to scream,
Suddenly I wake up,
The dream passes by.

Joe Stone (10)
Staplehurst School, Staplehurst

Superpowers

Spider-Man shoots webs like a spider.
When Hulk gets mad he annihilates stuff.
Wolverine slashes and dashes all day.
The baddies come along.
Oh no, it's Rhino.
He's mad like a lunatic.

David Brown (10)
Staplehurst School, Staplehurst

Dance

D ancers in bubbles of air.
A ll so excited for the day.
N ever done before but all so fine.
C alling everyone in the crowd.
E very week all living the dream.

Freya Marie Lawrence (10)
Staplehurst School, Staplehurst

You Can Be

Famous is what you are
An actor is what you can be
A magical dancer is what you can do
Oh wait,
That's just me,
Beep, beep, beep, beep!
Another day...

Billie Kennedy (10)
Staplehurst School, Staplehurst

My Nightmare! Ah!

M any people have this sort of dream.
Y oung people get scared of this.

N ever enter an alleyway.
I n the night especially.
G irls will scream, maybe boys too.
H e is there, the crazy clown.
T ales say that he will kidnap your siblings.
M aybe he has taken my sister because she is gone.
A fter, he turned up with a gun.
R unning, another man turns up.
E verywhere he said, 'Do you want to play a game!'

A fter, I woke up to find piercing red eyes at the end of my bed.
H a, I woke up in my bed, crying.

Jolie-Mae Brown (11)
Sundridge And Brasted CE Primary School, Sundridge

Dream Into Nightmare

I walk along the green glossy grass,
My family clutch my silky hands,
The sun shone brightly
On the beautiful meadow beyond,
I stare longingly at the hundreds of stunning rainbows.

But then, suddenly,
The sun crumbles into a pile of burnt ash,
My family slowly disappear from sight,
The rainbows turn black and grey
Like a miserable day.

Frightened I turn round,
The counting sheep are now snarling red-eyed hounds,
Exotic, multicoloured birds grow twisted horns
And fiery scales,
Flames flare up as high as the moon.

Screams resonate around me like howling wolves,
Blood trickles down the now dead valley streams,
I shut my eyes
And clear my mind.
Everything goes black.

Panting, I wake up in my normal bed,
I'm safe!
I'm alive!
I'm home!

Connor Savage (10)
Sundridge And Brasted CE Primary School, Sundridge

Hairy Legs!

I fell asleep in my warm cosy bed
Argh! Spiderwebs everywhere
This is not going to end well for me
Mud surrounding me
The sky was black
I could feel horror everywhere
I couldn't stop thinking
About what could be in the woods
Trees were covered in blood
I saw a spider.
Then loads more just came
I was scared
Brm! Brm! Brmmmm!
Argh! There standing just in the mist
Was a psycho holding a chainsaw
I ran as fast as I could
I could see a light
I got to it, I was free
Wait, not just yet...
A big mother spider came down from its web
And tried to kill me

I found a metal pole and whacked it
As many times as I could
Until it fell and died
And I, made it out alive!

Lewis Noble (10)
Sundridge And Brasted CE Primary School, Sundridge

Magical Monsters

M agical things surrounded me
Y awning stars awakened
T he fairies followed the adventure
H ills and trees
I cy lakes throughout
C akes with legs are chasing me
A dventures upon
L iquorice trees

C rawling creatures
R unning monsters started to growl
E ating bugs and birds
A liens and monsters threatened me
T eeth clattering
U nusual creatures racing
R evolting things I don't want to see
E els swimming in lakes
S creams followed me.

Maddison Mayo (9)
Sundridge And Brasted CE Primary School, Sundridge

Hope And Dreams Alive?

I am a dancer and my skirt is twirling,
On stage is the perfect way to express,
Ballet shoes tapping and hands pointing up,
The star of the lights shining.

Then I show my voice,
Singing my heart out through the night,
Pop, rap and classic,
The star of the lights shining.

Next I act to the camera,
Sassiness, sadness and socialising,
Is this a dream? I am with Emma Watson,
The star of the lights shining.

I experience the fame and finally
Become the star of the lights shining.

Jessi Johnson-Mills (11)
Sundridge And Brasted CE Primary School, Sundridge

Night

Up in a dark night,
Standing on grey clouds above,
This is a real fright.

I float, going for
The stars overhead, the light,
Below there's a car.

Down I sleep, soundless,
Wind blows around me,
I fall, feeling thoughtless.

I dropped into blackness,
Drifting in the abyss, I screamed,
The car screeched and stopped.

My parents looked back,
'Are you alright?' they asked me.
'Yes, I'm fine,' I said.

Luke Griffiths (11)
Sundridge And Brasted CE Primary School, Sundridge

The Monster

I watch you sleeping
A smile across your face,
Unicorns jumping and bouncing
Happiness is bad.

There are lots of dreams like this
All happy,
With superheroes, nice creatures and the future
Happiness is bad.

The corruption of nightmares
It may be sad,
But it will give you flashbacks
Happiness is bad.

There are little dreams like this
All sad,
With villains, evil creatures and the path
Sadness is here.

Dylan Roberts (11)
Sundridge And Brasted CE Primary School, Sundridge

The Worst Nightmare That Has Ever Been

N ever before have I been in a place so gruesome
I n this land there are monsters lurking out of the shadows
G rass has turned a lifeless ash colour
H ideous creatures waiting to gobble me whole
T he time has come, midnight
M ucus oozes from the dry leafless trees
A sound so creepy is all around me
R evolting witches' potions with monstrous ingredients
E ventually I open my eyes and...

Alfonso Oleo (10)
Sundridge And Brasted CE Primary School, Sundridge

Rocking

My mother is there
Holding me tight
Rocking side to side
Tears roll down her cheek
She hands me to my dad
His smile is as big as my head
I see through the window and this is hospital
I'm confused
This is strange
And wonderful
My dad tickles me
I laugh
And smile
And shriek
I let go
My dad passes me to my mum
She's laughing
She holds me tight
And rocks me to sleep.

Lily Coombs (9)
Sundridge And Brasted CE Primary School, Sundridge

A Princess Is What I Dream

A princess is what I dream.

P rincesses live in a royal castle.
R oyalty gets whatever they want.
I n a room full of tidiness.
N othing is impossible.
C an't stop thinking about my new true love who is waiting for me.
E ventually I will find him.
S top, I hear something.
S top, I see myself back at home safe in my own bed.

Molly Stubbings (10)
Sundridge And Brasted CE Primary School, Sundridge

Spiders In The Night

S cared, silent, no one around
P lease someone help me, wait - what is that sound?
I n the shadows above me I saw something move.
D amn my life, why is it so cruel?
E nthusiastic spiders drop from the ceiling like flies
R escue me, someone! This is my worst nightmare times five!
S uddenly, I wake up with a sick feeling in my head.

Mitchell East (10)
Sundridge And Brasted CE Primary School, Sundridge

Night Of Terror

Dark clouds around fluffy green trees
Surrounded as I get into the middle of the forest
Spiders crawling towards me
Bats swoop around as I try to call for help
But no sign.

I try to walk on but a woman in a witch robe
With blood all over and holding a chainsaw
Comes towards me.

What do I do?
I am alone... then I wake up.

Jaime Belchamber (10)
Sundridge And Brasted CE Primary School, Sundridge

I Dream

I dream of a field filled with happiness,
I dream of a monster climbing,
Monsters to mythical creatures,
A dream has a meaning,
You can be falling into the abyss,
You can be flying through the sky.

You will never get to the end,
You will never have another breath.

I'm lost in my dream,
I'm lost,
I'm lost...

Maddox Keen (10)
Sundridge And Brasted CE Primary School, Sundridge

Nightmares

N ervous and scared I wait for the kids -
I mpression that I'm fine - I give
G asping with the largeness here
H ealing, my glasses
T umbling near me.
M y knee, my knee
A pain, a...
R oughness.
E nd.

Jessica Dunmore (10)
Sundridge And Brasted CE Primary School, Sundridge

Desert Nightmare

I sit on the yellow sand,
Looking up at eyes that are red,
The sky is black and bland,
What awaits me, I dread.

I feel like I'm asleep,
But this can't be a dream,
I sit there trying not to weep,
Seeing a demon, the red eyes so mean.

Poppy Leigh (11)
Sundridge And Brasted CE Primary School, Sundridge

Life Of Death

Ghosts trickle up from their haunted graves,
A globule of blood from the stairway,
Zombies' arms hang from the brutes,
Staircase lets me go up,
My gran's shot dead,
No one is here,
I am dead,
Wake up,
Fine.

Harry Enrique Gullett (9)
Sundridge And Brasted CE Primary School, Sundridge

The Football Dream

There once was a boy who dared to dream
That he was the star player of his favourite
football team.
He was standing on the pitch, the crowd were cheering,
The opposing team was booing and jeering.
The whistle blew and the ball was up in the air,
He kicked it with skill and flair,
In came a tackle which left him on the floor.
But he didn't care, he just wanted to score
So he picked up the ball and placed it on the ground.
He took a deep breath and his heart began to pound,
He took two steps back to give him some space.
And with lightning speed he ran at the ball with pace,
He kicked the ball with an almighty force.
Where did the ball end up?
In the top corner of course!
In a few seconds the crowd looked surprised.
The boy felt happy and showed it in his eyes.
Suddenly he noticed everything began to fade.
The official football dream he made.

Lea Ehui Manalang (9)
Tubbenden Primary School, Orpington

Dreamy Weather

Drip! Drip! Drip!
The thundering rain splattered viciously on the pale window, desperate to get in.

Flash! Flash! Flash!
Lightning struck powerfully onto the innocent pylons, that towered over the damp street.

Roar! Roar! Roar!
The lion-like thunder raced through the extravagant waves in the grey blanketed sky.

Splash! Splash! Splash!
The thick coated mud lashed violently against the bladed grass.

Squirm! Squirm! Squirm!
Desperate to escape the gushing rain, earthworms burrowed their way through the soaked soil.

Slurp! Slurp! Slurp!
The snails - their slimy trail being washed away as they slithered along - tucked themselves into their patterned shells.

Creak! Creak! Creak!
Just then, the door downstairs began to widen.

Step! Step! Step!
Unwelcome footsteps edged towards my bedroom upstairs.

Boom! Boom! Boom!
My heart, a racing, lethal drum, pounded to the steps of this mysterious stranger.

Thud! Thud! Thud!
The unknown fled to the stairs and rapidly raced up, leaving squelching mud prints behind.

Creep! Creep! Creep!
In a blink of an eye, nature's eerie breath was still and the thuds had come to an end,
although I could still hear tiptoes echoing off my walls perpetually.
Heart thudding, oxygen losing, chest pumping, mind throbbing...
The lurking mystery creaked the door open and...
'Darling, get ready for school! We are not going to be late... again!'
Jumping out of bed, my bed hot and red, I then realised...

Joella Binns (10)
Tubbenden Primary School, Orpington

An Act Of Valour!

I'm at school doing my work
When suddenly a commotion takes its place.
Here and there in the city it lurks.
Only I have to meet it face-to-face.

As I transform, my mind is racing,
That this is what I have to do.
I'll jump out and say, 'I have no problem facing
A brutal enemy like you!'

As I fight and fight, I think and think,
If what I'm doing is right.
As I fight and fight, I think and think,
Until my enemy gives me a fright!

One of the people is holding a knife,
In my mind I make a note,
That with that knife, that very knife
He will slit my very throat.

A small, cold fear enters my heart,
But I'm courageous, I have nothing to fear,
He counts to three and makes a start,
And before long he is very near.

Then I count to three and take a leap,
And I reach for his black top hat,
I grab it and land on my feet,
And the hat? I tear that.

Then I, smiling to myself, captured the source,
And I glance sideways at the man.
It was a hard course,
My enemy has turned into a harmless man
And he says I've got millions of fans.

Feeling proud and well I hide and transform back,
And I walk back to my place.
My teacher is relieved to see me come back
With a smile on her face.

Niranjanaa Vijayakumar Sangeethaa (9)
Tubbenden Primary School, Orpington

A Witch Entertainment

Putting ingredients into the bowl,
Gathering piles of black misty coal,
Stirring cautiously the witch peered,
It was too sour as she had feared.

Mixing in green legs of frog,
They had been gathered from a damp bog,
Next was a tongue of lizard,
Which belonged to a noted wizard.

Enormous eyes of an eagle,
Soon she'll add tails of a beagle.
The time has finally come,
Just checking if it was done.

Bang! Pop! Now a fizzle!
Whoosh! Boom! Then a sizzle!

Luminous red, majestic blue,
She really liked it and you would too!

Just one finishing touch,
Not too many, not too much.
Tipping in the edible glitter,
Not too sweet, not too bitter.

Secret ingredients fading away,
The magic smoke starting to play:
'As the coherent spells reveal
All the potions shall conceal!'

The perfect potion blasted in one flame,
It's nobody's fault, so who's to blame?
With a grin she swivelled her hands.
Then, soared off to foreign lands.

Don't go away,
That was just today!
But for tomorrow,
A new beginning will follow!

It has risen: The marble moon.
That means she'll meet you soon.

Joana Francesca Tunaru (9)
Tubbenden Primary School, Orpington

Penalty Shootout Dream

Standing here I can hear as they shout and cheer,
When I turn I can see 100,000 people staring at me.

I am in Nou Camp,
The match of the year,
El Classico - Barcelona vs Real Madrid.

My heart pounds with anxiety,
My blood pumping thick and fast,
The pressure is real as I do this task.

My teammates surround me;
Messi, Neymar and Iniesta,
A nod of the head eases my nerves
From a teammate and a friend.

With the sun beating down from the bright blue sky,
Beads of sweat trickle down my neck,
As I step up to take the shot.
Silence falls throughout the stadium,
I can feel the eyes watching my every move.

My right foot touches the ball,
I hold my breath in anticipation as the ball curls,
Bang! The ball hits the back of the net.

The crowd roars and everyone jumps to their feet,
The adrenaline pumps through my veins
With pure exhilaration.

I never want this moment to end!

Tyler Gallacher (10)
Tubbenden Primary School, Orpington

This Is A Nightmare

Creaking floorboards and haunting screams,
Buzzing switches and roaring cars,
Punching gunshots pierce my head.
This is what a nightmare sounds like.

Iron doors and stony cave walls,
Dangerous dragons and orange ogres,
Come to get you with fire and axes.
This is what a nightmare looks like.

Giant waves of slime in a sea of vomit-like green,
Waxy leaves in a man-made forest,
Stroking the back of your neck.
This is what a nightmare feels like.

Sweaty socks and rotting waste,
All come together in a stinking race.
Attics and dust are a must
To frighten me out of my skin.
This is what a nightmare smells like.

Bland, brown and yellow,
Bananas all gooey, mushrooms all muddy,
Sandy and gritty, gloopy and pukey,
This is what a nightmare tastes like.

But when I'm tucked up in bed,
Holding onto my ted,
I'm in my world of joy.

Danny Kennedy (8)
Tubbenden Primary School, Orpington

A Unicorn Dream

I was dreaming about a unicorn
That waved its long pink hair.
It twirled its bottom and shook it in the air.
I never thought I would see one
But now I had the chance.
I liked to see it dash around the grass,
I always had a glance.
It gleamed at me so I gleamed back.
It looked like it was going to charge,
So I decided just to be nice
And give it a good old stroke.
I'd never thought that unicorns
Had a swirling white horn
That pierced through her heads,
Because that's cool.
My feet shuffled through the luscious green grass
That made a squeaky noise.
I was very suspicious about what happened,
But then I realised it was Unicornland.
The sky had fluffy white candyfloss clouds
Surrounding each and every part.
I had a very good relationship with the unicorn

So we decided to become friends.
So, after all this dream was really real,
I can't believe it was true.

Chelsea Boateng (9)
Tubbenden Primary School, Orpington

Candyland

When I go to sleep I dream a funny dream.
It is a dream you would never think of.
You would never think of this
But it is about candy,
Now there are lots of different candy,
All sorts of sizes and shapes,
They can also be colourful too.
These candies were bright in every way,
Some can be swirly or funny shapes,
Now you know most people like candy
But you would only come here
If you have a really sweet tooth.
All candy is sweet and colourful too,
The most colourful candy there is, the swirly pop
Everyone wonders what the toffee light
Would be made out of.
So they are made out of different coloured candyfloss.
What are the houses made out of?
The houses are like
What little girls and boys make for Christmas,
So gingerbread houses.

All the people there are gummy bears
And jelly babies,
So this is Candyland, my dream.
Dream big and let your imagination run wild.

Daisy Dennis (8)
Tubbenden Primary School, Orpington

Good Dreams, Bad Dreams

I fell onto my bed,
I snuggled up with Ted,
Fairies and dragons, which one would I choose?
Where would I start to search for clues?
Neverland or the Cave of Doom?
Candyland or the witch's Castle of Gloom?
Plants or leaves on the trees?
Insects or buzzing bees?
Left or right, which way would I go?
Would I be fine or would I get stuck in snow?
I decided to go to Candyland,
Which way would it be?
Would I go through a door or should I find a key?
Would I find a castle?
Would I find a cave
Or would I find a beach so that I can bathe?
I decided to go left, it looked very nice,
Until I got to the end of the road
And I was in a world of ice.
Who would I see?
Would I see my twin self
Or would I see a horrible mean elf?
Was it a good dream or was it bad?
Fall back to sleep and don't be sad.

Isabelle Rose Stother (9)
Tubbenden Primary School, Orpington

The Cactus Jack Nightmare

(Poem inspired by the film 'Curse of Cactus Jack')

I saw a film called Cactus Jack
That night I had a dream he came back

Jack was a greedy, selfish man
Who searched for gold with his pan
He found lots of gold, big and small
But Cactus Jack kept it all
He bought clothes, drink, food and more
He never spent any on the poor.

Jack died alone with all his gold
But his story is not fully told
Jack set a task before he died
He left maps and clues and many tried
People searched to find his gold but no one did
Until two young kids found the treasure he had hid
If they were greedy and took it all
Jack had set a trap to make them fall.

They discovered all that glitters is not gold
Being selfish and mean just leaves you cold.

Jack's bony hand moved in my dream
The nightmare woke me up with a scream!

Ava Prong (8)
Tubbenden Primary School, Orpington

There's A Witch In The Attic

There's a witch in the attic.
I saw her last night.
She gave my dog, Tom, a terrible fright.
How long has she been up there?
When will she come down?
She always has a smile
But she grins like a clown.
Her hair is bright green
And on top of that
Is the sooty black shape
Of her pointy witch's hat.
Her cloak is purple.
It runs down her back.
Her shirt hides in shadows,
Her shoes are pitch-black.
She smells like burnt sprouts
And mouldy old cheese.
I think I'll lock her in
And hide the keys.
I lie there in bed listening
As she squeaks like a bat
And cackles away
To her little black cat.
I opened my eyes

Then sat up in bed
The attic is a place
I will forever dread.

Teagan Foley (8)
Tubbenden Primary School, Orpington

My Super Dream

In my bed I drift off to sleep
And then I have a dream.
It's the same one time after time
I'll tell you what I mean.
I dream I am a superhero
My name is Super Strong Joe
I'm dressed in black with an orange mac,
I fly super fast, never slow.
Over trees and houses
Super Joe flies across the sky
I soar above the birds and planes,
I can fly so very high.
I can run as fast as a cheetah
Faster than the speed of light
I can wrestle any villain
They will never win the fight.
I fought off the criminals
I saved the day
Everyone shouted, 'Hip hip hooray!'
When I wake up I'm back to me
All cosy in my bed
But I'm still super,
That's for sure,
Well that's what my mum said.

Joe Harvey (8)
Tubbenden Primary School, Orpington

Fiery Unicorns

They breathe fire, turning trees to ash.
They have fur like fire
And manes that burn light streams.
If fire spreads nothing can be saved,
Everything precious gone.
The unicorns disappear never to be seen again.
I still believe in them, no matter what people say,
They're fiery unicorns, my unicorns forever,
To this very day.
But one cold day, fire appears.
It's them, the unicorns,
I meet them and greet them
But it happens again.
Fire burns to the ground,
Cameras flash as the news arrives,
They run,
They have nowhere to hide.
I help them escape,
They run.
I never see them again.
My eyes fill up
With tears tumbling down my cheeks.
Sadness swallows me,
They are gone forever.

Beth Smith (9)
Tubbenden Primary School, Orpington

Sandman Dreams

S leep steals over the world in a scare
A bove cities, dream thoughts swirl like a plasm
N ebulus tendrils of dream reach out to new location
D ark cave halls ring and echo underground
M ythical realms steadily rush past in a stream
A rising city, legend reborn, full of life Atlanta
N eptune's gases swirl and bubble like a cauldron

D esert sands, windswept, battered, torn and rugged
R ainforest birds swooping like a pretty jewelled dancer
E choing valleys sing then hum back in praise
A ndromeda far away, a glimpse of whirling panorama
M inutes fade, time forgotten, lost in the dream
S leep slips away, day breaks, the world awakes.

Helen Scarlett
Tubbenden Primary School, Orpington

Famous Spiders

F amous spiders scuttling up the carpet so proud
A midst shouts and screams from the crowd
M aking their way to the stage, posing as they go
O ut to make an impression at the big show
U tterly fantastic: different colours, different sizes
S ome of them will surely win prizes.

S uddenly a striped cat comes miaowing all around
P ouncing and screeching - what a terrible sound
I magine the chaos the cat manages to cause
D abbing at the spiders with her huge paws
E scaping the clutches of the frightening furry beast
R apidly running in every direction - north, south, west and east
S uddenly I wake with Kiwi the cat on my bed.

Oliver James Russell (8)
Tubbenden Primary School, Orpington

Dino To Dragon

There was once a dinosaur
That was so tall it would squash
The ones that were too small.

It would roam and stomp and terrorise the land
Oh this dinosaur thought it was so grand.

But day by day his nightmares raced towards him
Faster and faster
Oh no, it was becoming a massive disaster.

From that day he had excruciating pains
On the sides of his colossal body.

Week by week,
Every dinosaur would back way further and further.

One terrible day two enormous wings
Had grown from his back.
His wings were so big and strong,
They could make hurricanes across the earth.
Suddenly he could burn what he wanted
He had become a monster.

Mason Grieve (9)
Tubbenden Primary School, Orpington

Once Upon A Dream

Once upon a dream I was lying in my bed,
With all these memories swirling in my head.

I remember being taken to a magical land
Where unicorns were playing in a big brass band.
Fairies sat giggling and making glitter beams
And I sat there thinking how beautiful this seems.

Pink flamingoes sang enchanting songs
And I felt like this was a place I really could belong.
I danced all night long with the new friends I'd made
Wishing and hoping this dream will never fade.

But so my dream ends with a happy bow
Because a beautiful dawn is starting right now.

The sun has risen and it's time to get out of bed
But my wondrous dream will always stay in my head.

Lexi Marchant (7)
Tubbenden Primary School, Orpington

Lost One Day

I was in the park one day,
When my mum walked away,
I was lost in the park,
Till it was very dark,
At night the park turned into a zoo,
And all the animals were staring at you,
There was a tiger, his stripes were red,
He had eyes on the top of his head,
There was a lion with a purple mane,
But I didn't stop to ask his name.
I saw a blue kangaroo,
Who said, 'How do you do?'
I walked for a while,
When I saw a laughing crocodile,
I was really scared, I started to run,
Where oh where was my mum?
All of a sudden I was in my bed,
Was it all in my head?
'Mum, Mum,' I started to scream.
'Don't worry, it was just a dream.'

Natalie Kentish (7)
Tubbenden Primary School, Orpington

Cherry Blossom Dream

Cherry blossom on the trees
Swaying in the slight breeze
It says things that we don't know
But we hear it in the glow
On the branches a bird perches; a finch
It moves, but just a pinch
The twigs twine and twirl
Just like a ballerina's swirl
A little girl climbs the trunk
When she falls she doesn't cry,
Instead a cheeky grin spreads across her freckled face.
The bright red cherries,
Like drops of blood in the sky
Are sweet on the inside, ironic isn't it?
The cherry blossom stands so still,
So perfect, just like how we will never be.
It still stands there waiting and waiting,
But who is it waiting for?
We shall see...

Tanvi Venkatram (10)
Tubbenden Primary School, Orpington

My Candy World!

In my Candy World, there are marshmallow clouds and candy cane trees.

In the magical rainforest, the vines are made out of strawberry laces and the rocks are jelly beans.

Houses are made out of toffee and everybody loves to drink milkshakes, because nobody likes coffee.

The moon is a ball of candyfloss, that lights up the sky at night.
Everybody travels in chocolate cars and planes.
Candy World is a lovely sight.

Evie Eliza Seri-Ross (8)
Tubbenden Primary School, Orpington

Hospital Views

Soon I was there in a hospital room
I was so lonely and so full of gloom

Bricks all the time here and there
Soon I'll have bruises everywhere

But Mum was there beside my shoulder
And she said, 'You'll be OK, you're getting older.'

Then soon it was time for bed
Did the evening schedule and then I read.

The next day I saw a monstrous machine
This can't be true, I need some caffeine!
What does this mean?
And there I was, in the room again
No more problems with my brain.

Free to go home, on my own
No more sad views from my hospital window
With a healthy body home I go.

Tiago Ward (10)
Tubbenden Primary School, Orpington

The Olympic Gold Medalist Final

Whizzing through the runners' brains,
Like there were planes just flying everywhere.
All of a sudden, there was a false start;
I was running as fast as possible.
Then the other runners looked back,
And saw me catching up.
Rapidly, I sped past them at speed;
And then I was away.
There were still three more laps,
By the time, they started lap two I was half a lap ahead.
I lapped them all and then I was on my fourth lap.
I charged as fast as I could towards the finish line.
I finished and waited for them to do two more laps.
Eventually, they finished the race.
After the race, I got the gold medal and a gold trophy;
For the fastest runner ever.

Anthony Louis O'Shea (8)
Tubbenden Primary School, Orpington

Someday Maybe

Someday, one day
I will leap to the stars and even stand on Mars,
I will become a great poet
And want the world to know it,
I will become a purple cat and purr on the mat,
Someday, one day.

Maybe, maybe
I could run a million miles in just one tap,
I could even be an explorer and find an old map,
I could be a famous diver and dive off the ten,
I could win lots of medals and beat a million men,
Maybe, maybe.

In my world I can see...
A secret garden with sweetie trees,
A massive room with a piano and a big diving pool,
A big poster with pictures to be drawn,
In my world I can see all my friends!

Charlotte Bloodworth (8)
Tubbenden Primary School, Orpington

A Present

A present was delivered to my doorstep,
But there was no one there
And I had a scare,
It was a bear.
I ran around my house, going up and down,
Around and around.
There was only a stamp
And a bold logo on the top.
I opened the present but nothing was inside
Except a tiny guinea pig.
It was not much bigger than a fat rat,
So I fed it a milk bottle and it tasted like silk.
I thought it was just a normal guinea pig
But it wasn't.
It could turn into anything so he wasn't normal
So I went to Pall Mall to sell the guinea pig.
After all of that in my head,
I closed my eyes,
I was home in my bed.

Mattea Kathryn Emily Blue (7)
Tubbenden Primary School, Orpington

The Lost Beautiful Mermaid

There was a mermaid called Nixy
She ruled over the sea
One day a wizard took Nixy away
And locked her up
She tried to use her magic
It didn't work
But she was royalty and beautiful
Clowns guarded her
Because the wizard wanted to marry her
One night, when everyone was asleep
She quickly grabbed the keys
Suddenly she was lost
What to do, she wandered around
Then she found an old mermaid
He gave Nixy a ball of superpowers
She looked inside, there were all kinds of powers
She tapped one and she asked to get home
She turned around
He disappeared so she followed where he went
She came home.

Laya Madhanagopal (8)
Tubbenden Primary School, Orpington

Raindrops

I wish I was a raindrop, as I saw it in my dream,
And I fill the world with flowers, purple, blue and green.

I wish I fell on mountains, which is full of barren trees,
I wish I fell on forests,
Which has thirsty animals scream.

And make them full of colours,
And make them full of life,
Berries and buds which blossom,
Creepers, vines and leaves.

I will travel with the clouds
And play with the mighty sun
And frighten kids with thunderstorms, wind and fun.

I wish I was a raindrop, I saw it in my dream,
And fill the world with flowers, purple, blue and green.

Shlok Verma (8)
Tubbenden Primary School, Orpington

Champions League Final!

S tepping on the pitch
A nd looking around
N ow it was my time to shine
T urning around I look at the fans
I feel the atmosphere running through my veins
A nd then the match begins
G oing for the ball
O ur team attacks.

B ale passes down to me
E veryone awaits a goal
R oars from the crowds begin
N ow the ball whips in the goal
A nd I run celebrating
B ut that leaves us only one-nil down.
E veryone cheers and then we score, the match was won
U ntil then, I found out it was only a dream.

Christian Kukushev (8)
Tubbenden Primary School, Orpington

Out In Space

I stare out of the window and gaze into the sky,
And as I do that I wave the Earth goodbye.
This is the steering wheel and this is my small seat,
Which is where I always must be tucked in neat.
I barge into a room that lets out all the air,
But when I open the door I see a large bear!
Wow, how big it is, totally bigger than me...
But then I see an even bigger bumblebee!
Then I see another one and another one,
Finally I see the last one, guess what?
It is eating a bun!
'Is this a dream? Are bears in space?' I say,
Then I open my eyes wider
To find I'm safe in bed!

Maria Lenyova (7)
Tubbenden Primary School, Orpington

Legend

F inally I arrive, this is where legendary dreams are made.
O n the green velvet pitch I stand, waiting for my moment to come.
O nly legends have stood where my feet stop.
T oday is the day where a new legend rises. Everyone is counting on me.
B ravely I place the ball on the famous penalty spot.
A ll eyes on me as I stand back, I take a deep breath and shoot...
L egend! The ball smashes through the keeper's legs.
L ying on the pitch I look up at the sky. The crowd chanting my name. Today a hero has risen. I am the new legend of football.

Harry Stirling (8)
Tubbenden Primary School, Orpington

The Tiger

It all happened when I was asleep.
I could not hear a single peep.
I saw some tigers near the fence over there.
They were chasing shadows here and there.
I was looking over the fence as happy as could be
But someone got in my way, I could not see
So I climbed the fence feeling brave.
A boy was watching, looking rather grave.
That's when it happened, I felt myself slip.
I fell into a mud-filled pit.
A streak of orange, a flash of black,
I fell on my back.
I saw its long sharp teeth glistening in the sun.
Suddenly I woke up to the sound of my mum.

Mia Anderson (8)
Tubbenden Primary School, Orpington

The Magic Horse

Here I am in my dreamy garden
Looking at my horse, Emalarden.
And there she shows me her magic wings,
And up we fly as she sings.
Emalarden takes me to a magic land,
A lot of flowers growing in the sand.
I saw a sign saying: 'Welcome to Heaven,
All are welcome from seventy to seven'.
There were fruits from strawberries to lemon,
Extraordinary mangoes and lots of melon.
I actually had so many friends:
Melanie, Ellie, Joana, Simon and Dan.
Just two hours later I had to go,
I was sad and full of woe.
I remember waking up to reality instead!

Imani Ward (7)
Tubbenden Primary School, Orpington

Sweet Dreams

My mum says goodnight and sweet dreams,
My eyes start to close and I drift off to sleep.
I feel a picture coming close,
I open my eyes into a dream.
I take a step forward and stare into the distance.
I can see the colours and oh so much more.
Colourful candy as far as I can see.
I take a mouthful and walk into a world of candy.
The candy queen says, 'Take whatever you please.'
I couldn't believe it,
I did everything there was to do.
Suddenly, I woke up in my bed,
Excited for the next night ahead,
Hoping it will be another sweet dream.

Olivia Ann Huntingford (8)
Tubbenden Primary School, Orpington

Dangerous Dragons

D rooling dragons crawl around and beside that they
never even have a frown.
R ooming and brooming all around, when people see
him they scream, 'Let's all get out!'
A ngry dragons scream with pain and the people say,
'Hip hip hooray!'
G roaning dragons sit aside and all they are thinking
of saying is, 'Bye-bye!'
O minous dragons give a sign but all they want is just
to learn how to fly.
N umerous dragons set free and all they say is bye-
bye.
S izzling and zooming all around but now the humans
have a frown.

Faris Shawah (9)
Tubbenden Primary School, Orpington

I Wish I Could Be A Footballer

I was deep in sleep
Far, far away
In a field as far as you can see
There were loads of football players
I wish I could play
To show them my skills
To be a star
To know how it feels
Then someone called, 'Hey you!
Do you want to play?'
I was feeling surprised
What could I say?
I ran to the team
And kicked a ball
I skilled up a few people
I felt really tall
I ran in the box
And I took a shot
I scored a great goal
I enjoyed it a lot

I really am a star player
I thought.

Lucas Cossar (7)
Tubbenden Primary School, Orpington

Dancing Dream

D reaming that I'm the best dancer in the world
A spin, a kick and a jump
N othing is as exciting as this
C rowds cheering and waving for me
I feel like a star as I dance on the stage
N arrow dance shoes tighten as I twirl
G littering lights shine in my eyes

D aring leaps as high as the sky
R ehearsals are over, if I want to win
E very step I take brings me closer to my dream
A pplause are all around me
M inutes seem like hours as my dream finally comes true.

Cara Richardson (9)
Tubbenden Primary School, Orpington

Fear

They're stuck in your head,
You'll wet your bed,
Your eyes well up with tears,
They surround you now, getting out, it's your fears.

You...
Hear...
The...

Sounds of screams,
They echo near,
They're the opposite of your dreams,
It's your scary fear.

You...
See...
The...

Glowing red eyes,
Their body's black coal,
Your parents... they told you lies,
Yours is the last... they have found your soul!

You meet the same fate as the rest!

William Edmundson (10)
Tubbenden Primary School, Orpington

I'm A Little Fish

I am a jolly fish that lives in the sea.
Many different colours all around me.
I feel so happy and free
With so much space to swim and play -
It's my favourite place.
I have lots of fish friends
That live in the sea with me
But they always think of having me for tea.
My favourite thing is to be a fish
I just wish I wasn't such a tasty dish.
I'm getting trapped in a fishing net
And it is very wet.
I think I'll stay here forever
But I am very clever.
I will call my friend
He will save me in the end.

Emily Isherwood (7)
Tubbenden Primary School, Orpington

Famous Football Spiders

Two famous spiders ready for their next match,
Their names were Steven and Jose,
They were the best of the best,
They lived high on the dirty gutter.

One summer's day, they decided to have a match,
They worked and scored,
Neither of them won,
It went into penalties,
They stopped fighting about who's the best player,
They became friends.

They went on holiday,
But unexpectedly the spiders were killed by the bears,
Their wives gave birth, it all started again,
And will keep going on forever.

Henry Pink (7)
Tubbenden Primary School, Orpington

My Magical Unicorns

The glittery rainbow horns twist
And turn gracefully in the moonlight.
Shiny eyes scan the mysterious room
Like a bright torchlight.
Silky, wavy hair, brushing past her long neck
While the crimson red sun rose.
Magic unicorns floating around in my head.
I imagine them to be as peaceful,
Calm and as free as a beautiful bird.
The dream was unforgettable.
The light hooves press against my feather-like pillow.
As the light breaks through my window.
My alarm bell rings
And I'm excited to see what the day brings.

Daisy Eloise Hemming (9)
Tubbenden Primary School, Orpington

In The Wild

From behind the golden cornfields,
A cloud of dust arose,
Buried amidst the herd,
My mane streams out aglow,
Ears are pricked, nostrils flare
When a sweet smell comes through the air,
A trickling of water and a spring comes into view,
Flowers blooming, tree trunks looming,
A carpet of fallen leaves, home to a nest of bees,
Wind whistles, ruffling the hedgerows,
The day has come to an end,
Ribbons of moonlight stream, all through the night,
Like a fish on a hook,
It holds back the greeting of the morning light.

Imogen Spear (9)
Tubbenden Primary School, Orpington

Where Will The Fairies Take Me?

Where will the fairies take me?
Hmm, let me think.
Will they take me to a magical place when I blink?
Will it take me to a place
That will put a smile on my face?
The fairies with their shimmering wings
Dancing around me and make me sing.
With their houses made of mushrooms
And the glittering lights
I can see them shining
Through the darkness of the night.

The fairies are my friends,
I love them with all my heart.

And every night, I say goodbye,
We will never be apart.

Emma Poppy Sene (9)
Tubbenden Primary School, Orpington

The Big Bad Wolf

My blood is cold like ice,
This feeling is not nice.
He is going to eat me up alive,
Will I ever get to be five?
He is not going to catch me this time,
I am looking for a big tree to climb.
I've reached the top, it's time to hide,
When the wolf is gone, I need to slide.
I quickly run to my bike,
But I hear a sound I do not like.
It is a howl of the Big Bad Wolf,
I cycle home which is to the north.
Oh no! The wolf is lurking straight ahead,
Then I wake up safely, all tucked up in bed.

Isabel Stow (7)
Tubbenden Primary School, Orpington

Team Raptor

Raptor 1 is the fastest of them all
As fast as the wind
He hunts for his prey.

Raptor 2 is all about teamwork
Helping his friends when they're in trouble
Planning attacks when they are hungry.

Raptor 3 is all about surprises
Stealthy approaches, clever tactics and pounces!

Raptor 4 is the most fierce
Grinding and cutting through his prey
Not caring who's in his way.

Then a T-rex comes to devour them,
But he is in for a surprise...

Jack Isherwood (9)
Tubbenden Primary School, Orpington

Midnight Mayhem

Midnight mayhem spreads the streets,
Listen carefully, hear the shrieks.
You may have heard some spooky noises,
Telling you some freaky choices.
So get under your bedcover
And be prepared to be scared,
Because you will find some bony figures
Eating up your lovely bed sheets
And even you!
Oh no! So run away into the deserted streets
Here dead zombies fly above you
Where skeletons looked silly but gross,
You may have to hide to not be found
By the worst people in the world. Oooohhh!

Olivia Grace (7)
Tubbenden Primary School, Orpington

Rainforest

Once upon a dream...
I found myself in the rainforest,
I saw the birds swimming in trees,
I saw frogs and fairies flying
And I saw the dancing bees.

I saw a phoenix flying in the water,
I saw a crocodile nesting on a hippo's head,
I saw a fly flying without wings,
I saw a sheep resting on a flowerbed!

As I walked further in the rainforest,
I found a sparkling, snowy desert,
I screamed with astonishment
And I woke up and found myself in bed!

Ansharah Azfer (8)
Tubbenden Primary School, Orpington

Fairy Dream

Fairies do seem
Like a dream
As they flutter all day
As they may
Through the lovely warm weather
Because they're so clever
Although they flick their sparkly wands
Above the glistening ponds.
If they giggle
They're surely being tickled
Through the summer
They listen to loud drummers
And they play
Throughout the warm summer's day.
As they flutter,
They eat soft butter
Whilst they pick pretty flowers
Near the tall, rusty, old towers.

Jessica Demi-Ejegi (7)
Tubbenden Primary School, Orpington

My Dream

When I was small like a little baby,
I once had a dream about big Georgie Davey.
When I grow up and grow big and tall,
I really want to play football.
When I get older I want lots of things
Like flashy sports cars and diamond rings.
When I get older and get superpowers
I will fly around for hours and hours.
When I get older I will quickly run
And I will have lots of fun.

Now you have heard my dream as a little baby,
This is the story of big Georgie Davey.

Georgie Davey (8)
Tubbenden Primary School, Orpington

The Unicorn

U nder the cover of night, I can see your shimmery mane.
N earer and nearer I get to the land of unicorns.
I feel the magic tingling around me, as I reach out to your silky white body.
C antering around the fluffy clouds, I feel that nothing can stop me.
O n my majestic head I see your golden horn.
R iding you makes me feel that anything is possible and dreams do come true.
N ow morning creeps into view, my image of you is fading, until next time.

Eleanor Smith (9)
Tubbenden Primary School, Orpington

The Fire-Breathing Cyclops

Crotchety and furious,
the enormous fire-breathing cyclops
sprinted through the Earth's core.
Yellow and red flames came burning on his boiling hair.
Curious and strong he smelled the blood of children.
Licking his lips he imagined
the sweet, crunchy taste of children.
Over the scorching hot stones
he dug towards the surface.
Panting he reached the village of Fogo.
Striking fast he grabbed twenty-six children
and had them in a sandwich with pickled onions.

James Charleton (8)
Tubbenden Primary School, Orpington

Why Did You Go?

Unicorn, unicorn, where did you go?
We're really stuck and we do not know!
If you have a secret,
You know we can keep it!
We can't find you in the long, long grass,
Hopefully, not too much time will pass,
I think we've found you under the tree,
We're not far away from the deep blue sea,
Do we need to find something that you have lost?
Is it covered in pearly frost,
Unicorn, unicorn, why did you go?
I don't think we will ever know!

Annaleese Butler (10)
Tubbenden Primary School, Orpington

My Dream

I dream in multicolour.
I dream of paintbrushes and pants.
My brush brings life to my dreams.
As the colours touch my canvas.
The golden cottage with the red door
In the spring meadows I dream.
The garden is the meadow in my dream.
In springtime the meadow comes alive with butterflies.
I fly with them as the dazzling river flows
Along with me in my dream.
I see pink and purple roses in the meadow
Oh how I dream, how I dream.
Come and dream with me.

Rosalind Burgon (7)
Tubbenden Primary School, Orpington

Supernatural Powers

I wait for eyes to close
And mind to reach dream state
And then the magic begins.
I stand up on my window ledge
And stretch my arms out wide
I jump and then I'm flying high up in the sky.
Tonight I'm flying to a distant land
Where fun can never end.
My journey takes me past the moon and stars
Through the night I go, having fun
As the eight hours draw to a close
I make my way back home
What fun adventures I have had
Flying on my own.

Daniel Mundy (8)
Tubbenden Primary School, Orpington

My Dream About School

Going to Tubbenden is pretty neat
Because of all the people I get to meet
My friends and teachers are all in one place
Which helps to put a big smile on my face.

Every day I come to school
The days are fun and really cool
Miss Fowler makes our lessons great
Even when I'm a little bit late.

Spellings are hard but maths is fun
And during play I skip and run
School is all about work and play
And I enjoy going every day!

Olivia Lily Rose Hunter (8)
Tubbenden Primary School, Orpington

Dark Feelings

Feeling melancholy,
The sensation of devastation engulfs me,
Ebony black, a cloud of distress,
Swirling around, is all I can see,
A piercing pain wounds my broken heart,
Inflicting my body with a searing strain.
The look on your face, that look of horror,
Will never depart from my agonised brain.
My fists are clenched and my fingers are scarred,
I lost a fight, against myself.
I wake up, suddenly and am curling in bed,
Like my usual self.

Patrick Williams (10)
Tubbenden Primary School, Orpington

The Dream I Had Last Night

Last night I had a dream that made me smile
But it went on for quite a while.

It involved a unicorn
And it had a lovely horn.

There was also a wizard, evil and scary
He was also very hairy.

The unicorn showed me Candy Land
We even saw a gingerbread man.

I made lots of friends
But this is all where it ends.

The wizard appeared and before I could turn my head
There I was, back in bed.

Ruby Hancock (10)
Tubbenden Primary School, Orpington

Astronaut

Off we go to space, we'll win the race.
Blast! We are going really fast.
I am feeling very bold, but it is also very cold.
We need to avoid the asteroid.
I have on a silver suit, with great big boots.
We're on our way in the Milky Way.
Flying through the stars, on our way to Mars.
Travelling into the dark, in our super space ark.
Heading into the black, we need to stay on track.
Round and round the moon, we'll be back home soon.

Thomas Dedman (8)
Tubbenden Primary School, Orpington

The Hat-Trick

As I enter the stadium I see the cheering fans,
They are waving claret and blue flags in their hands,
The match is going well,
I have just scored my second goal,
And then I get a penalty for a West Brom player's roll,
I kick it with my left foot and it flies into the net,
And now I've scored a hat-trick,
This is my best match yet,
The fans are all cheering and really going wild,
I've always had this dream ever since I was a child.

James Faulkner (8)
Tubbenden Primary School, Orpington

Dreamtopia

D reamtopia is a wonderful place
R emember all the adventures you face
E mpty your mind and drift away
A s well as doing quests today
M arch across deserts, fly across seas
T o reach your destiny in your dreams
O pen your mind, see animals and plants
P lanets and stars doing a mystical dance
I mpossible is not a word that exists
A nother dream is upon us so let's do this.

Micah Porter (7)
Tubbenden Primary School, Orpington

A Dancer's Destiny

Dancers around me sob and shout,
People running all about,
I watch them all fight,
All day and all night,
I stand there helpless, in fright,

Slowly I start to dance,
The music touches my heart,
I spread the joy of music all around,

They stop to sob and shout,
People stop running all about,
I watch them stop their fight,
Make old and new friendships become right,

This is my dream.

Aashna Goyal (9)
Tubbenden Primary School, Orpington

My Pet Dragon

My dragon is blue and can breathe fire too.
He roasts my marshmallows
In place of campfires
And breathes air into my flat bicycle tyres.
He protects me from bullies and flies
Upside down but the funniest thing
Is he is as silly as a clown.
He slips on banana peels,
Trips over sticks
And gets his tail on fire
When trying to perform tricks.
My very own dragon;
I love him so,
Especially the way his eyes glow.

Kai Muguna (8)
Tubbenden Primary School, Orpington

Wishing Star

W ishing star, wishing star up, up, up so far
I like it, you like it, lovely wishing star
S o how far do you go?
H igh I'm sure
I would like to put a bow on you
N ot a T-shirt
G o, go, I'll wish a wish for my best friend

S tanley! My best friend appears
T ammy! My friend appears
A nna! We were all together
R osha! And we all watched the star.

Lilly Christine Knight (7)
Tubbenden Primary School, Orpington

My Christmas Dream

Every night when I go to sleep
I have the same dream,
It always repeats.
I see myself dressed as an elf
Dancing under the Christmas tree
Ready to have a shopping spree
But then I hear jingle bells
And I think I'm under a spell
Then I wake up with a start
And I realise it was all in my heart
Because I love Christmas
Even though it's only spring
It will all still come true
And to this I will sing.

Manon Dominois (8)
Tubbenden Primary School, Orpington

Summertime Dream

S ummer is awesome, you can play all day.
U mbrellas have been put away
M ost people like to go to the beach
M arvellous fruits grow like a peach
E veryone has a fun time
R unning dogs love playing in the tide
T imeless days with lots of fun
I nteresting colours start the fun
M usical summer madness where everyone sings
E xcited people sing different things.

Isobel Mary French (10)
Tubbenden Primary School, Orpington

Superhero

I dreamed a dream
Where everything gleams.
I can jump super high
And I can fly across the sky.
I'm a superhero who catches people for their crimes.
I must catch them all in time.
I wear a big red cape.
It's so bright you can see it from the sky.
A superhero never lies.
His superhero dog is never far
They're good friends,
They always save the day
Especially in the month of May.

Charlie Ashton (8)
Tubbenden Primary School, Orpington

Argh!

Argh!
Am I in a nightmare?
Me and Ruby lost in Dragon World.
I see a big dragon.
He sees me
He starts to run,
Argh!
Stop naughty dragon
Run Ruby, run!
Scared and frightened
Ruby is frozen.
Runnn!
Stop naughty dragon
He wants to eat us.
Run!
He is super-duper fast.
I can't keep going.
Argh!
The dragon runs quick
But we run quicker.
Phew!
We lost him.

Isobel Taylor-Jones (8)
Tubbenden Primary School, Orpington

Diplodocus

D angerous with his big long tail
I ncredible long neck that can reach so high
P lenty of trees to fill his appetite
L oves to munch on juicy leaves
O h how huge this creature is
D arting above pterodactyls fly
O h how far he roams this planet
C *lump, thump, clump, thump* he goes
U nbelievable size and power
S tomps about as he takes each step.

George Birch (10)
Tubbenden Primary School, Orpington

Shooting Stars

Luminous stars shot in the ebony black sky,
Wishes were formed on this special night.
I was fast asleep as dreams filled my mind,
Suddenly I woke up to find my wish was created
over night.

As I crept downstairs in the morning light,
I could feel the excitement, would it lead to delight?
I looked at the table and standing there,
Was a beautiful birthday cake for us all to share.

Madeleine Porter (9)
Tubbenden Primary School, Orpington

Dinosaur's Lunch Menu

Dinosaur, dinosaur, where have you been?
Having my lunch friendly fiend
Crunching and munching
Sucking the juicy blood.

I see, but not so much
I stomp through the tangled trees
Look around carefully and patiently then
Jump out and devour my prey.

Can I see your teeth dinosaur?
Yellow teeth, he gets closer
Bloodstained, he gets closer
Then, *chomp!*

Shaurya Kadian (8)
Tubbenden Primary School, Orpington

Unicorn

Unicorn, your eyes shine bright,
You follow me throughout the night.

Unicorn, your muzzle is soft,
Through my dreams your images waft.

Unicorn, your strong wings beat,
Slowly I sit on your soft, soft seat.

Unicorn, your long legs thunder,
As we gallop I quietly wonder.

Unicorn, your wild tail swishes,
Your arrival grants my luxurious wishes.

Rosina Staggs (9)
Tubbenden Primary School, Orpington

Catching A Big Fish

If I could have one wish
It would be to catch a big fish
I fish with Daddy all the time
With a rod, reel and fishing line
I sit on the bank out in the sun
Waiting to catch a special one
Fishy, fishy, where are you?
One as big as a house will do
My alarm goes off, my rod has a bend
Here he is, my fishy friend.
He's in my net weighed, a photo too,
Thank you fishy, you will do!

Amy Sawyer (8)
Tubbenden Primary School, Orpington

Creepy-Crawlies

I was in bed
I thought I heard a buzzing in my head
I opened my eyes and my feet were not there
I had to stop and stare
I couldn't believe my eyes
And to my surprise
Wasps were in front of me
But they were having tea
I thought it was not right
It gave me an awful fright
Before I knew it
I gave the wasps a hit
Check out your window to see
You may meet a bee.

Isla-Siobhan Brown (8)
Tubbenden Primary School, Orpington

My DJ Dream

I like to be noisy and play my music loud,
I dance to the crazy beat and shout out to the crowd,
My flashing lights and glitter balls light up the room,
While my bouncing speakers go boom, boom, boom!
People clapping, cheering, asking for more,
I sing into my microphone for the encore,
Happy people are boogying as the crowd goes mad,
I'd love to be a DJ, it's the best dream I've had.

Henry West (8)
Tubbenden Primary School, Orpington

My Sweetie Land

Walking down the jelly bean lane
Surrounded by mountains of candy canes
There I see in front of me
Gummy sweets dancing so merrily
I stroll down the path
And there I notice some chocolate flowers just for me
You can gobble them up with one bite
They're so tasty so be careful how many you take
A marshmallow castle towers over me
And a lollipop says, 'Good morning darling!'

Abigail Williams (8)
Tubbenden Primary School, Orpington

Unicorn

U nder the clouds lived an unbelievable unicorn.
Unaware of her.
N atural beauty. Nearby the narrow and noisy road
let her
I magination run away with her, she had an idea.
C almly she checked her colourful clothes and
O utdoors it was, free from the barn, able to
R un wildly under the beautiful rainbow.
N obody to answer to, just another unicorn.

Summer Rae Hattley (7)
Tubbenden Primary School, Orpington

Nightmare

G etting lost was scary
E verything seemed strange
T ime took forever
T o get back to my friends
I felt lonely and emotional
N ot knowing where I was
G oing round in circles

L ooking for someone I know
O ver there, where I first came from
S uddenly I see
T wo of my best buddies - yippee.

Evie Shave (8)
Tubbenden Primary School, Orpington

I Dream, I Dream

I dream, I dream
Of what I could be, a professional footballer
Is what I see.
I hope and pray to play at West Ham one day.
On the pitch with Carroll, Cresswell and Lanzini
Are the best players I would say.
The grass is green and the goals are white.
We win the cup with all we fight.
They put us to the test
But we are the best.
Oh West Ham, I dream, I dream.

Ashton Bignell (8)
Tubbenden Primary School, Orpington

A Dragon Poem

My dragon has eyes as round as dinner plates.
It has sharp teeth like daggers,
Its mouth is dark and wide like a cave.
It has claws which are as pointed as needles.
Its nose lets out plumes of smoke
Like a chimney.
Its body is as huge as an ocean whale.
Its tail flicks from side to side
Like it's an angry cat,
It sits silently waiting to catch its prey.

Abisan Vigneswarm (7)
Tubbenden Primary School, Orpington

Dragons

Long, long ago, in the stories of old,
The dragons were brave, the dragons were bold.
The dragons flew over the village below,
Dragons' hot breath did glow.
The princess up high in her tower
And the dragons below try to devour.
Knights in their shiny armour
But the prince was much more of a charmer.
Dragons in their caves,
The knights were very brave.

Tyler Smith (8)
Tubbenden Primary School, Orpington

My Nightmare

Sometimes I have a nightmare
Like the one I had last night
About a gigantic barn owl
Who gives me such a fright

He grabs me with his large claws
He pulls me out of my bed
He flies me above the forest
Now I'm really scared

The owl eventually drops me
I fall through the sky
I land safely in bed
And then I wave goodbye.

Niamh Leonard (8)
Tubbenden Primary School, Orpington

The Fairy

Come back fairy, I miss you,
Fairy wings that shimmer so bright.
With sparkles and fairy dust
Shining like diamonds throughout the night.
Visit us again soon little fairy
And make my wish come true.
I will wish upon a star
Just to get a visit from you.
Where are you and how do you feel?
I wish you would turn me into a seal.
Bye-bye little fairy.

Ella Lynch (7)
Tubbenden Primary School, Orpington

Magnificent Class

T aking you on a ride to my dream class
E verybody so happy to be in PE on the smooth grass
A t the end of the lesson the bell for break rings
C alculating for me as my students go down to the
playgroup to sing
H appy it must be to be outside
E veryone isn't so trapped inside
R aining heavily as my students sing inside.

Micah Assim (8)
Tubbenden Primary School, Orpington

Dreams And Nightmares

Delightful dreams lead to happiness and laughter
When you're asleep your dreams are so exciting
You can't wait to go to sleep
To see what happens.
Magical things happen when you're asleep
It could be leading onto a nightmare!

Terrible but exciting things happen
When you're asleep.
Can't wait to see what's next!

Emily Rose French (10)
Tubbenden Primary School, Orpington

Are Fairies Real?

A fairy in the sky stood there just like a dragonfly.
It glowed bright with beautiful wings
Like a butterfly.
Was it really a fairy?

I couldn't believe it, I saw a fairy in a sandpit.
The stars shimmered while the fairy's wings glimmered.
The fairy cascaded down from the height
And I realised they were fireflies.

Tingxuan Huo (8)
Tubbenden Primary School, Orpington

Sombrero Man

His hat glimmered in the desert,
He eyes the black figure in the foggy sky,
Frustrated the Burkatron
Zoomed towards Sombrero Man,
For days they fought extremely viciously,
The crowd watched in horror
As they saw Sombrero Man
Fight Burkatron to the death,
Finally Sombrero Man won the fight.
Burkatron was defeated.

Anna Charleton (9)
Tubbenden Primary School, Orpington

Fire-Spitting Dragons

Fire-spitting dragons
Flying through the sky
Flapping their wings
Way up high.

Chasing scared people
Making them run away
Fire-spitting dragons
The terror of the day.

Knights in shining armour
Come and save the day
Fire-spitting dragons
Knights will come to slay.

Kai Hollesen (7)
Tubbenden Primary School, Orpington

Candy Land

Houses of gingerbread, towers of candy canes
Trees of lollipops, skies of ice cream
Sheep of cotton candy, bears of gummy jelly
Roads of strawberry laces, cars of bubblegum
Pools of maple syrup, fountains of chocolate
It's time for candy, it's time to eat
The land I dream of is a land of candy!

Dylan Harrison (7)
Tubbenden Primary School, Orpington

Becoming A Footballer

F irst I saw myself
O n the football pitch
O h what a goal I scored
T alking to myself
B eing famous, yay!
A nd everyone knew me
L uck is always with me
L earning every day
E nding matches with hooray
R eady for the future...

Tim Vladimirov (8)
Tubbenden Primary School, Orpington

Dreaming Of Dogs On The Beach

I see dogs running swiftly across the blue shiny water.
I am laughing excitedly
I hear dogs splashing in the huge waves, leaping about
I am ecstatic
I smell salty dogs swimming in the sea peacefully
I am elated
I love when dogs dig joyfully
In the soggy sand for bones
I am overjoyed.

Eve Ellis (7)
Tubbenden Primary School, Orpington

Beach Dream

By the sea is where I like to be
Especially with all of my family.

We dig holes and build sandcastles
Until the day is through.

When the sun goes down
We all go home.
That's when I think to myself,
I can't wait to be back by the sea again.

Alfie Mitchell Mauri Hattley (9)
Tubbenden Primary School, Orpington

All About Me

I dream...
I am a boy
Who likes to play
With trucks and toys
Every day

I'm always at school
Except at weekends
When I act cool
With some friends

One day I grow
I'll be a man
I'll drive a car
And play when I can.

James Drew (7)
Tubbenden Primary School, Orpington

Dream Land

I am on a unicorn,
High above the clouds,
Looking around all I see
Are big pink trees,
I saw an enormous brown griffin,
Sitting on a grey rock,
It gestured the unicorn down,
I got onto the griffin,
It soared high above the trees,
To my lovely home.

Louise Kentish (8)
Tubbenden Primary School, Orpington

Where Did You Go Fairy?

Come back fairy
Are you lost?
Did you go looking for a bunny
Or are you being a boss?
Please come back
I miss you
Have you got your backpack?
I hope you do.
Where did you go?
Please tell me
Now I know
You're riding a bee.

Hannah Pearson (10)
Tubbenden Primary School, Orpington

Unicorn

U nicorns live in Candy Land.
N eed to eat crushed, hard candy.
I would like to join them to eat
C andy as much as I can.
O h sweet unicorns.
R ainbow colours everywhere.
N othing can look more shiny.

Arya Bilger (8)
Tubbenden Primary School, Orpington

Killer Clowns Nightmare

Killer clowns with bombs.
Killer clowns with axes.
Killer clowns with knives.
Watch out for them!

Killer clowns with dangerous bombs.
Killer clowns with dangerous axes.
Killer clowns with dangerous knives.
Watch out for them!

Kelsey Pink (9)
Tubbenden Primary School, Orpington

Unicorn!

Unicorn come back, where are you?
Are you looking for a rainbow
Or are you being a boss?
Please come, I miss you,
Have you got your case?
I hope so, where did you visit?
Please can you tell me,
Are you flying through the midnight sky?

Sophie Louise Martin (10)
Tubbenden Primary School, Orpington

A Mixed-Up Poem!

Footballers are kicking the ball
Dinosaurs are stomping over all
Dragons roaring over schools

Heads are higher
Feet are lower
The sky is lighter

Tails are swinging
Fire is flicking
Boots are kicking.

Oliver Blaney (8)
Tubbenden Primary School, Orpington

I Was Driving

I was driving in a Nissan that's shiny gold.
I went up the hill, down the slope.
Round and round the roundabout,
Left, right and left again, *stop!*
There right in front of me was my family
Waiting for lots more...

Izzah Qureshi (8)
Tubbenden Primary School, Orpington

A Wizard's Tool Kit

A loyal, trusted wand waiting for its order.
A bright, magical spell prepared for its victim.
A fluffy, gracious owl soaring through the sky.
A fast, nimble broomstick making gutsy spins.
Beware of the wizard!

Emily Franklin (10)
Tubbenden Primary School, Orpington

Mysterious Eyes In The Eerie Night

R unning at the same speed as a sabertooth cheetah.
U ndercover secret agents.
N othing and no one can stop them.
N o joke.
E nders...
R unning to come and get you!

Marshall Washington Mitchell-Dale (10)
Tubbenden Primary School, Orpington

Rugby Hero

D aring drop goal at the Rugby World Cup Final
R oaring crowds
E cstatic moment
A wesome game
M an of the match
S igh - I dreamed I was a rugby hero.

Daniel Amor (8)
Tubbenden Primary School, Orpington

The Disaster

One day I went to Dan's house with Mason and Alfie
We did a video,
Then a big portal came into the room,
It was shining like the moon,
We jumped in and realised we were in Minecraft.
All of a sudden we saw Herobrine
He came for us,
We fought back, just with our fists.
We won, then ran,
Now we were so tired of running,
We were like thirsty pigs.
We met a fellow traveller, his name was Liam.
We asked him,
'Do you know the portals?'
'Back to the real world of mortals?' he replied.
We realised he was a guy
Who rhymed all the time.
He was so boring that I was snoring.
But he tricked us
He put us into the Nether portal!
We quickly jumped out and we were free,
Suddenly, I woke up, it was a dream.
I got out of bed and stamped on my dad's tool,
Oh no, it was time for school!

Finlay Paice (9)
Valley Invicta Primary School At Holborough Lakes, Snodland

My Friend And The Dog

One day I decided to go on an adventure,
So I called my friend to join me,
Then we went to a random planet
And we arrived at Dog World
And made an assignment to see who would help
And join us.
One dog called Bella,
Who is a pug soldier wanted to join us,
Then we decided that she should join us.
Then we left,
'We had a message that someone is in danger,
In the castle in the deep, dark forest.'
'OK,' said Bella.

30 minutes later...

We arrived at the castle
And barged into the house and there were two ogres.
Their faces were as ugly as a witch's.
The ogres slashed their sword, *bang, crash.*
They missed us.
'Quick,' I said,
Then when the sword cried, 'Why did you hurt me?'
He wept to the ogre.
When the ogres were concentrating on the sword

We ran past them.

10 minutes later...

When we got past all the guards
We saved the princess and she said,
'You took so long...'
And before she finished her sentence
I used my magic to destroy her.

Sometimes I use my powers for good or evil,
It's just if I'm in the mood.

Mason Boorman (10)
Valley Invicta Primary School At Holborough Lakes, Snodland

The Ork Raiders

There was an army of orks
Ruled by an evil king,
They had a bloodthirsty nature
And a terribly poisonous sting.

Their empire was enormous,
They ruled Saturn, Jupiter and Mars,
Earth was their next target
And all humanity would be behind bars!

The ork raiders spotted a rocket,
Flying around the solar system,
Then the ork raiders flew,
Yelled the evil king, 'No! We missed 'em!'

But the ork raiders didn't give up,
They were determined as they pelted,
They breathed out a blast of fire
And then the rocket melted!

The ork raiders mounted their dragons,
They got off their dragons on Earth,
An ork dropped a black crystal,
But they didn't know what it was worth!

They had invaded Russia,
Next their target was Wales,
They had mounted their dragons again
And they were swinging their scorpion tails.

However the UK were allies,
That was what the orks didn't know,
A volcano erupted
And the king was shot down low!

The king was battle wounded,
He fell into the lava pool,
Oh no! I've woken up
And now it's time for school.

Liam Austin-King (10)
Valley Invicta Primary School At Holborough Lakes, Snodland

When I Press My Button

Ding! I pressed the button
And whispered,
'I want a horsey please,
A horse, so soft like a pillow.'

Ding! There it is in front of me.
A soft horse so cute.
I thought I was going to faint.

Ding! I pressed the button again
And I spoke, I wanted an adventure
To meet some monsters
And so I closed my eyes,
There I was in the monster's land,
There I met a soft, kind monster
Chatting to his friends.

We ate super delicious cake
And played lots and lots of games
Like pass the super noisy parcel,
Glance for the super, super angry
And naughty elf
And one more game called naughty hide-and-seek.

I was enjoying it so much that
When I looked at the clock,

It was monster time.
Ding! I pressed the button
And there I was,
At home dreaming such wonderful dreams.

Emilia Drwiega (8)
Valley Invicta Primary School At Holborough Lakes, Snodland

My Dream World

One night I was in bed when I closed my eyes
And went to sleep
And then in my mind I saw a little house,
It was coming towards me.
It started getting bigger and bigger until...

I saw a blue path right between my legs
So I walked on and on and then I was there.
I saw big trees the shape of lollipops.
I ate little flowers that were covered in milky
white chocolate.

I saw three people coming to me,
Suddenly I noticed they looked familiar.
I went closer and closer,
It was actually my family.

They had so much money,
There were two big bags and one little bag.
It looked like it had £999.
We went back home to spend the money on
magical things.
Sshh! Don't tell! Keep it as a secret
And it will last forever.

Mya Jarosova (9)
Valley Invicta Primary School At Holborough Lakes, Snodland

Got Lost In The Forest!

The trees are swaying side to side,
It was getting ginormous and even louder and louder.
Bang, crash, wallop, there was silence.
I didn't know what to do.
I was stuck.
A dragon dashed and came out of the trees,
It was scary.
I never knew this was going to happen.
The dragon's eyes were as red as fire,
So bright it hurt my eyes.
The car raced away from the dragon.
When the car sped away steam came billowing
out of the engine.
The dragon jumped in surprise.
He walked away sadly stamping his feet
As he thought they could be friends forever...
Suddenly the car went too fast
And tumbled down the hill.
Bang, crash, wallop!
I woke up feeling weak from my dream.

Caileigh Anne Shorthouse (9)
Valley Invicta Primary School At Holborough Lakes, Snodland

When I Press My Button

When I press my button
I can feel or I can be.

When I press my button I can be...
A beauty therapist working hard.

When I press my button it makes me feel...
Scared that my clown suit gets invaded by ghosts
And comes to get me.

When I press my button I can be...
A kind, loving child who's loved.
A kind, little monkey who's proud to be.

My button is fashioned in...
Galaxy paper and Once Upon a Dream
Emblazoned all over.

Boom!
I wake up
Wishing it is not a dream
But there is no button to be seen.

Ellie Emma Lusher (9)
Valley Invicta Primary School At Holborough Lakes, Snodland

Dreamland

A baby pink and baby purple galaxy
With little silver sparkles.
I saw unicorns prancing and dancing.
The flowers that surrounded us were as red as lipstick.
A pink castle was floating on candyfloss.
Shiny diamonds were glistening in the sky.

We were shopping 'til we drop.
Pink fish dancing in the still lake.

The white glittery unicorn made me speechless.
My rose-gold Disney castle glittering in the light.
My best friend, Torin, riding her unicorn, her face alight.

She rode out into the glistening galaxy,
The world fading as she rode away.

Ella-Louise Paige Hollman (10)
Valley Invicta Primary School At Holborough Lakes, Snodland

Monster

M *ash, crunch, stomp,* I heard a strange sound
O h I spotted a sign that said: *Out Of Bounds.*
'N o!' I said to myself, there was a big rip in the fence.
S *ob... sob,* I started to cry, there was a huge monster!
T he monster started running towards me as I
climbed through the part in the fence...
E agerly I ran into the forest, I got stuck on a bush
R *oar!* He was coming closer. I started to push
S uddenly I found myself on the floor... It was a
dream!

Vincent Johnson-Twomey (8)
Valley Invicta Primary School At Holborough Lakes, Snodland

The Big Shiny Moon

In a dream far, far away I am round
And sailing away.
Colours going inside my eyes.
I can't see anything but the bright colours in my eyes.
In the distance far, far away there is a sparkling moon
In the high distance.

How it is true and where am I?
Down below my little house lay.
How scary it is for me.
All the time my adventures go,
I can always see the moon
Wherever I am at night.

Under the night sky I walk around,
I finally know what has happened to me,
I wake up from my nice dream.

Oliver Yates (8)
Valley Invicta Primary School At Holborough Lakes, Snodland

The Black Stallion

The tree clanged my back as I galloped,
I kicked my behind legs in the air,
Through the thorny forest,
His hooves like a lion roaring.

The ground was wet and calm,
I slipped into the river,
Cutting my shoulder on a rock,
I was dripping wet with dirty water.

When I finally reached the edge,
I could hear a crow croak.
In the distance I could hear an eagle
Soar over my head in the sunset,
The rising sun, the cry of people
And the sound of my house.

For I am the black stallion.

Scarlett Spalding (9)
Valley Invicta Primary School At Holborough Lakes, Snodland

World War II

I woke in the middle of Africa
In a strange hospital.

A sixty-year-old man nearby whispered,
'Your squad was ambushed.'
I had no idea what he was talking about.

My brain was sinking at the idea
That I was almost dead.

At this thought, I felt a shaking noise
And a lot of pain
Like somebody stabbing me.
I woke up on my bedroom floor.
My left shoulder blade was begging for care.
I looked onto my bedside table,
Saw a picture of my dad in the war.

Cade Steven Breytenbach (9)
Valley Invicta Primary School At Holborough Lakes, Snodland

The Dragon

It's over there,
Shh,
It might wake up,
Creak goes the floorboard under my foot,
Oh no,
OK, it's not awake.

The fire-breathing dragon
Who once stole our house,
Roar, argh! I hide, he can't find me,
Now I'm dead, he found me.
What, I'm in his stomach.

Wake up, wake up,
Suddenly something else is alive,
It's going to eat me,
It shows its fangs
And licks his lips,
At soon I wake safe in my own bed.

Katie Raggett (10)
Valley Invicta Primary School At Holborough Lakes, Snodland

Killer Clown

Thud!
There was a loud noise in the kitchen.
It hurt my ears.
I woke up, went down.
Suddenly, there was a laugh.
A killer clown.
He chased me all around the house.
He got me in a van.
I came out.
I was in an old house,
He trapped me for days.
After day 66 I came out.
I was in the woods.
I broke free.
I woke up and realised I was dreaming.
I woke up in such amazement.
Thank goodness it was only a dream.

Joshua Terence Graham (8)
Valley Invicta Primary School At Holborough Lakes, Snodland

Danger

The trees were as dark as space
So I took one step on and it felt weird.
It was still moving but I had second thoughts.
Then I saw something growing,
I ran to it but it moved,
It was a unicorn.
I asked it to take me around the forest
And it said yes.
We had fun until suddenly,
Thunder roared so I said, 'Fly,'
And it flew and he was grateful
So I kept the unicorn.
Suddenly I woke up, I felt weird.

Luke Millen (9)
Valley Invicta Primary School At Holborough Lakes, Snodland

Unicorn Fun

Once upon a dream
There was a unicorn.
Her name was Pegasus.
Her wings were as shiny
And sparkly as ever.
Her furry back was white as a cloud
But Pegasus always stood out in a crowd.
Pegasus was also very loud!
She lived with her brother, James.
They loved playing with each other.
Their favourite thing to do was chasing animals into the jungle.
Pegasus and her brother,
James hated being shouted at.

Rhys Ayrton Hollman (9)
Valley Invicta Primary School At Holborough Lakes, Snodland

Untitled

I saw that unicorn dazzling in the starry night.
I saw in her eyes,
The moon glittering with summer.

As she looked at me
I saw her twirly horn like rope.
Her mane was as pink and purple as the rainbow.

Her white nose was cuddling my cheeks.
We landed on the floor.
I woke up,
Thought it was real.
I still talk to her even now.
I think I can hear her whispering voice in my ear.

Paige Woolgar (8)
Valley Invicta Primary School At Holborough Lakes, Snodland

Football

F irst I fell asleep and dreamt I was a footballer
O n the pitch I run really fast
O h, I kick the ball so hard I can't miss
T he ball swiftly floats into the back of the net
B *oom!* Everybody cheers because I score
A ll the fans chant my name aloud
L uckily, the full-time whistle blows and we win
L ast month we won 2-0 against Millwall.

Jack Curtis (9)
Valley Invicta Primary School At Holborough Lakes, Snodland

The Dream Finally Happened

I can see fairies, birds and unicorns.
This is weird, I'm lost! Unicorns are following me.
I find a gloomy castle.
I enter a room that's bright with a flame-throwing dragon.
The dragon is as red as fire.
I come across a garden as big as a field.
The dragon is bursting with anger.
The dragon smashes a window.
The trees are sleeping in the rain
While the grey storm is screaming.

Mia-Jade Masters (10)
Valley Invicta Primary School At Holborough Lakes, Snodland

The Dream Of Horseboxes

I was having a dream that I had a huge, brown,
Glossy horsebox on my driveway.
All my friends came to see it.
My dog went in the horsebox.

I was just so happy that I had a horsebox
Worth £70,000 for my birthday.
Then I started to cry with excitement.

I woke up from my dream,
It wasn't real that I had an amazing horsebox
That everyone loved.

Francesca Lee (9)
Valley Invicta Primary School At Holborough Lakes, Snodland

Galaxy Glitter

I mounted the sparkling white unicorn
And I galloped off the rose-gold Disney castle with Ella.

We looked at the garden,
There were roses, as pink as blush
And topiaries shaped as unicorns and puppies.

We entered the glamorous castle
And had the most delicious sushi.

The unicorns were dancing
And prancing around us...

Torin Violet Harris Edghill (10)
Valley Invicta Primary School At Holborough Lakes, Snodland

When I Grow Up

When I grow up I want to be a teacher
And teach magical things.
To be the most amazing mum that anyone could be.

When I grow up I want to live in a mansion
And to have a friend to teach.

To have lots of children to teach
And be the head of my school.

I want to teach in Year 1
And teach them things they want to know.

Faith Turley (9)
Valley Invicta Primary School At Holborough Lakes, Snodland

When I Grow Up

I dreamed that I met a unicorn.
He was in a big, white, fluffy cloud.

I dreamed I met a princess,
I was in a carriage with the princess.

I dreamed my friend came round my house,
But when I woke up,
I didn't know that she was at my house.

I dreamed I was a teacher
And I had 100 people in my class.

Marlie Chenai Tree (8)
Valley Invicta Primary School At Holborough Lakes, Snodland

Dreams

D iving into the air, *whoosh!*
R acing the other humongous stunt plane
E veryone is excited and cheering to you on holiday
A icrafts with their massive wings soaring
M aking sure you have a safe flight
S ighing with your co-pilot ready to fly!

Kenley Groombridge (9)
Valley Invicta Primary School At Holborough Lakes, Snodland

Growing A Garden Of Sloths

Puff,
Trees are growing right and centre.
The growing magic dust really works.
My sloth will love a garden.
A tree so huge,
I climb and climb
But when I reach the top
There is a giant as kind as a bee.
He invites me in for tea.
Me and my sloth have tea with a giant!

Jaiden Spalding (8)
Valley Invicta Primary School At Holborough Lakes, Snodland

The Unicorn's Superpowers

Unicorn, unicorn
Where are your superpowers?
What makes you camouflaged
And what makes you fly?
In space you can't die.
Ten dragons see the powers.
They want the power
But the unicorn is magical.
They don't get it and never do.
Unicorn, unicorn
You are super.

Gene Anthony Stotesbury (7)
Valley Invicta Primary School At Holborough Lakes, Snodland

My Home

My home is as big as a volcano.
My home is orange and blue.
It flashes like lightning when robbers come near.
Inside the walls is every colour of the rainbow.
In one room of my house, there are piles
Of shining gold everywhere.
I love my home.

Samuel Reynolds (7)
Valley Invicta Primary School At Holborough Lakes, Snodland

Spiralling

Woah! What's this strange land I see?
Dragons and donkeys,
Dingos and drums.
The gossiping clouds and weeping rain.
This land is both weird and wonderful.
Eerie and exotic.
So... confusing!

Robyn Lee Harris Edghill (8)
Valley Invicta Primary School At Holborough Lakes, Snodland

Land Of Ooo

I woke up from my soft, squishy bed,
I looked in the mirror, I had a marshmallow head.
I looked out the windowpane
And knew I was not sane.

The clouds were like fluffy candyfloss balls,
There were lemon drop rain falls,
A candy cane streaming high,
Hundreds of gummy birds in the sky.

Some chocolate logs on the ground,
Five gummy worms in a mound.

Then I woke up from my bed
To realise it was in my head.

Finn Ashley Crane (11)
Wellesley House, Broadstairs

YoungWriters
Est.1991

YOUNG WRITERS INFORMATION

We hope you have enjoyed reading this book – and that you will continue to in the coming years.

If you're a young writer who enjoys reading and creative writing, or the parent of an enthusiastic poet or story writer, do visit our website **www.youngwriters.co.uk**. Here you will find free competitions, workshops and games, as well as recommended reads, a poetry glossary and our blog.

If you would like to order further copies of this book, or any of our other titles, then please give us a call or visit **www.youngwriters.co.uk**.

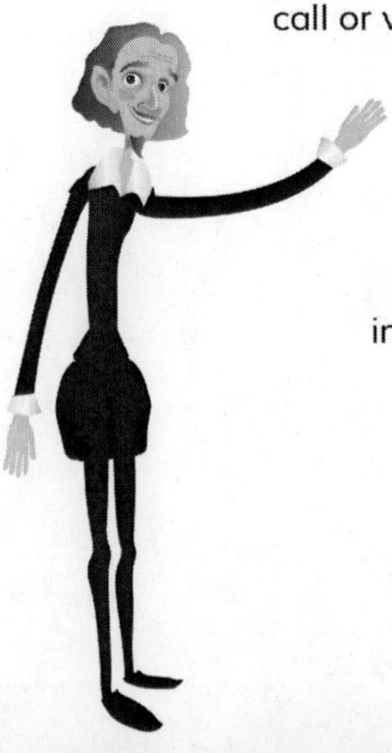

Young Writers
Remus House
Coltsfoot Drive
Peterborough
PE2 9BF
(01733) 890066
info@youngwriters.co.uk

Snakes in the wild

Cliff Moon

Wayland

In the Wild

Alligators and Crocodiles in the wild
Bears in the wild
Eagles in the wild
Elephants in the wild
Giraffes in the wild
Gorillas in the wild
Hippos in the wild
Kangaroos in the wild
Leopards in the wild
Lions in the wild
Pandas in the wild
Penguins in the wild
Sharks in the wild
Snakes in the wild
Tigers in the wild
Whales and Dolphins in the wild

Further titles are in preparation

This book is based on Venomous Snakes, *in Wayland's 'Animals of the World' series, by Bernard Stonehouse.*

First published in 1985 by
Wayland (Publishers) Ltd
49 Lansdowne Place, Hove
East Sussex BN3 1HF, England

ISBN 0 85078 519 7

Phototypeset by
Latimer Trend & Company Ltd, Plymouth
Printed in Italy by
G. Canale & C.S.p.A., Turin
Bound in the U.K. by
The Pitman Press, Bath

Contents

Snakes

Have you ever seen a snake?
You can see snakes in the reptile house in a zoo.
Sometimes you may see snakes like adders or grass snakes in gardens and fields in Britain.
But you would have to go to a hot country like Africa to see large venomous snakes in the wild.
Venom is a poison which some snakes use to help them kill an animal they want to eat.
The snakes in this book are venomous.

Puff adders are venomous snakes.
They live on the African plains and they are very dangerous.
They can be 2 metres (6 feet) long.

This is a timber rattlesnake.
Its fangs or teeth move forward
when its mouth opens and
the poisonous venom comes
from its fangs when it bites.
Snakes which do this
are called front-biters.

Green tree snakes live in Africa.
This one has caught a frog.
It holds on tightly until its venom
has killed the frog.
Then the snake swallows the frog
and slides into a quiet place
to digest its meal.

The Indian forest cobra rises up and spreads the hood which is on each side of its neck.

This black coachwhip snake is having a drink.
It is called a coachwhip because its body is like a thin whip.

Snakes are cold-blooded animals.
They become slow and sleepy
at night when it is cold but
when the sun warms them
they come out to hunt for food.

This African boomslang came out
and waited in a tree until
a chameleon came near.
Suddenly the snake grabbed
the chameleon and held on tightly
while it injected its venom.
The chameleon will be dead
in two or three minutes.

How long do you think
it will be before the snake
needs another meal?
(Answer on page 58)

Central American tree or vine snakes are back-biters which means that their venom comes from their back fangs. Back-biters usually eat food which will fit into their mouths and these vine snakes eat lizards most of the time.

This African boomslang has just
shed its old skin.
Snakes shed their skins
at least once a year.
The new skin is bright and shiny.

Snakes' Lives

There are about 3,000 different kinds of snakes that live all over the world. Snakes are reptiles but they do not have legs like tortoises and crocodiles.

Millions and millions of years ago there were lizards which lived in underground burrows. Their legs became shorter and their bodies became longer. Slowly these lizards began to look more and more like snakes.

Snakes often live together in warm holes or burrows. These snakes spent the night together and now they are coming out into the sunshine.

Most snakes are good swimmers and
their skin is waterproof.
This black cobra is keeping its head
out of the water as it swims
across a flooded field.

Snakes are well camouflaged.
They are usually the same colour
as the places where they live
and hunt for food.
So it's hard to see a snake
which isn't moving.

This sidewinder snake is moving
across the desert sand.
It keeps most of its body
up off the ground because
the sand is so hot.

Small snakes often move along
by curling their bodies and
pressing back against the ground
to push themselves forwards.
Large snakes keep their bodies
straight and glide forwards
by rippling their skin.

But what do snakes do when
they have to move quickly?
(Answer on page 58)

These are the scales on the skin of a puff adder.
All snakes have tiny scales like these which overlap or lie side by side.
Most snakes have scales which are beautifully coloured and patterned.

This pilot black snake
is shedding its old skin.
Snakeskin is strong and
some people like to have shoes
and handbags made from it.

A puff adder with her babies.

Sometimes snakes try to swallow animals which are too big for them. This young rhinoceros viper choked to death when it tried to eat a large rat.

Most snakes lay eggs. Here is an Indian small-spotted coral snake looking after her two eggs.

Food for Snakes

All snakes catch their food and swallow it whole. But how do they know when there is food nearby? They do not have ears but they can feel the sounds of animal movements. Which part of a snake's body feels the sounds?
(Answer on page 58)

A snake's fangs are long and thin so that it can hold on to its food.

African black mambas can be
3 metres (10 feet) long.
This mamba is waiting for
a bird, mouse or lizard
to come close.

A snake uses its tongue
to taste the air
as it moves along.
Snakes know from the taste
when food is nearby.
This timber rattlesnake
has pits below its eyes
which can feel the heat
of another animal.

Some snakes are brightly coloured like this coral snake which lives in the southern U.S.A.
The colours warn animals and people that the snake is very dangerous.

This flying snake has killed
a large lizard.
Flying snakes climb high
in the trees and jump
from branch to branch.

Snakes do not have eyelids but
they have a thin layer of skin
which covers their eyes.
They cannot see very clearly but
they can tell when something moves.
If you ever meet a snake
you should stay quite still
and if you are lucky
it may not see you.

This is a puff adder's head.
What do you think it has
in its broad cheeks?
(Answer on page 58)

A mongoose has killed this cobra.
The mongoose is one of the snake's worst enemies.
People also kill snakes either because they are dangerous or because they want the skins for handbags and shoes.

Birds such as owls, hawks and eagles kill snakes for their food. They swoop down and grasp the snake behind its neck so that it cannot bite them. Then they break or chop the snake into small pieces.

But snakes also kill snakes. Some snakes like North American king snakes live on other snakes. How do they manage to do this without getting killed themselves? (Answer on page 59)

Colubrids and Cobras

There are about 2,500 different
kinds of colubrid snakes—
the largest family of snakes—and
a few hundred of them are venomous.
They are all 'back-biters'.
They live in many countries but
most of the venomous colubrids
live in hot countries.

Cobras belong to another
large family of snakes.
This Indian cobra is spreading
its hood to make itself look
bigger and more dangerous.

This paradise tree snake
is a flying snake which lives
in south-eastern Asia.
It is a colubrid which catches
its food high up in the trees.

Montpellier snakes live in the
warm countries of southern Europe.
They can be 2 metres (6 feet) long and
they live on birds, rats, lizards
and other snakes.

Cottonmouth vipers are dangerous snakes which live in the swamps of the southern U.S.A.

This is a long-nosed tree snake.
Some tree snakes flatten their bodies
to make a sail when they jump
so that they can glide
through the air.

Most cobras live in India and the warmer parts of Africa, southern Asia and North and South America.
They are all front-biters and their venom is deadly.
How many people die each year from cobra bites in India?
(Answer on page 59)

African spitting cobras can spit their venom at enemies to frighten them away.
The venom is very painful if it gets in your eyes or nose.

Banded kraits are in the same family as cobras.
They have warning colours and a ridge along their backs.
They are very dangerous.

Mambas can kill people
when they bite.
This is an African green mamba
and it is looking for eggs
and small birds to eat.
Some mambas grow to be
more than 4 metres (13 feet) long.

Sea Snakes, Vipers and Rattlesnakes

Sea snakes live in the warm parts
of the Indian and Pacific Oceans.
They usually stay close to the shore
and they live on fish.
They come up to breathe but
they can stay underwater
for many hours.
Some sea snakes come on land
to lay their eggs and
bury them in the sand.
But some baby sea snakes
are born alive in the water.

This cottonmouth viper is opening
its mouth to attack.
Can you think why
it is called a 'cottonmouth'?
(Answer on page 59)

Sea snakes look for food along the sea bed.
Their venom will kill fish in a few seconds.
They wag their tails from side to side as they swim through the water.

This puff adder is well camouflaged among the African desert rocks in bright sunlight. Puff adders kill hundreds of people each year.

The pit viper gets its name
from the pits in front of its eyes.
These pits can feel the heat
of another animal.

Vipers do not lay eggs—
their babies are born alive.
British adders are vipers and
they have between 15 and 20
babies in the autumn.

Most vipers have long fangs which move forward when they open their mouths.

This horned adder is swallowing a large desert mouse.

Rattlesnakes have a rattle
on the ends of their tails.
The rattle is made from dried skin
and it makes a loud noise
even on dry sand.
This is a diamond-backed rattlesnake.

Rattlesnakes live in the warm,
dry parts of the southern U.S.A.
and they grow to about
1·5 metres (5 feet) long.
Their venom is very dangerous
and it can kill people.

What do you think
rattlesnakes usually eat?
(Answer on page 59)

What should you do if a snake bites you?
Try to remember what kind of snake it was and go to a doctor who will inject a serum to make you better.

A doctor is getting venom from this cobra to make serum for people who get bitten by a cobra.

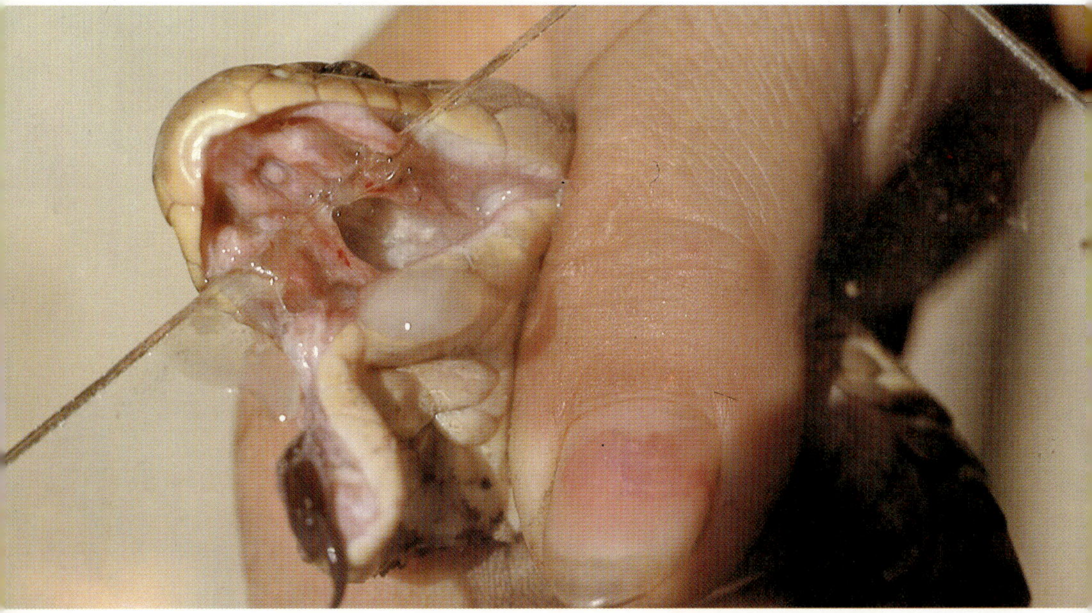

This copperhead snake has bitten the frog and now it is waiting for the frog to die.
Copperheads live in dry places in the U.S.A. and they sleep through the winter.
They are very dangerous.

Answers to Questions

Page 14
It will be several days before the snake needs another meal.

Page 22
When snakes have to move quickly they twist and turn so fast that they are very hard to catch.

Page 29
A snake feels the sounds of animal movements mainly through the bottom of its mouth.

Page 34
The puff adder has poison glands in its broad cheeks.

Page 37
Snakes like North American king snakes manage to live on other snakes without getting killed because they are not affected by their venom.

Page 45
About 10,000 people die each year from cobra bites in India. They are usually bitten when they walk bare-footed in the dark.

Page 49
Cottonmouth vipers got their name because their open mouths are white like cotton.

Page 54
Rattlesnakes usually eat mice, lizards and rabbits.

Index

Picture acknowledgements

All photographs from Bruce Coleman Limited, by the following photographers: Jen and Des Bartlett 8, 26 below; Rod Borland 23; Mark Boulton 15; John and Sue Brownlie 57; Jane Burton 20–21, 24, 35, 51; Peter Davey 30; Jack Dermid 42, 55; M. P. L. Fogden 12; C. B. Frith *front cover*, 27, 41, 43, 46, 52; David Hughes 53; Peter Jackson 38; Leonard Lee Rue III 10, 25, 31; J. Mackinnon 18, 33; Norman Myers *endpapers*, 11, 13, 17, 26 above, 28, 32, 36, 47, 56; G. D. Plage 44; Allan Power 50; Hans Reinhard 16, 40; John Shaw 48.